ROUTLEDGE LIBRARY EDITIONS:
HISTORIOGRAPHY

Volume 26

HISTORY AS A SCIENCE

HISTORY AS A SCIENCE

HUGH TAYLOR

LONDON AND NEW YORK

First published in 1933 by Methuen & Co. Ltd

This edition first published in 2016
by Routledge
2 Park Square, Milton Park, Abingdon, Oxon OX14 4RN

and by Routledge
711 Third Avenue, New York, NY 10017

Routledge is an imprint of the Taylor & Francis Group, an informa business

© 1933 Hugh Taylor

All rights reserved. No part of this book may be reprinted or reproduced or utilised in any form or by any electronic, mechanical, or other means, now known or hereafter invented, including photocopying and recording, or in any information storage or retrieval system, without permission in writing from the publishers.

Trademark notice: Product or corporate names may be trademarks or registered trademarks, and are used only for identification and explanation without intent to infringe.

British Library Cataloguing in Publication Data
A catalogue record for this book is available from the British Library

ISBN: 978-1-138-99958-9 (Set)
ISBN: 978-1-315-63745-7 (Set) (ebk)
ISBN: 978-1-138-64005-4 (Volume 26) (hbk)
ISBN: 978-1-138-64008-5 (Volume 26) (pbk)
ISBN: 978-1-315-63684-9 (Volume 26) (ebk)

Publisher's Note
The publisher has gone to great lengths to ensure the quality of this reprint but points out that some imperfections in the original copies may be apparent.

Disclaimer
The publisher has made every effort to trace copyright holders and would welcome correspondence from those they have been unable to trace.

HISTORY AS A SCIENCE

BY
HUGH TAYLOR

METHUEN & CO. LTD.
36 ESSEX STREET W.C.
LONDON

First Published in 1933

PRINTED IN GREAT BRITAIN

CONTENTS

PAGE

CHAPTER I

THE INHERENT CAUSE OF FAILURE I

Two main motives have contributed to the progress of the world, the desire to promote knowledge and the desire to influence conduct. These motives, however, are not found acting in co-operation but in conflict. In this conflict conduct has always been considered as of more importance than knowledge. The opposition between the claims of knowledge and of conduct is frequently reproduced in the mind of the same individual, generally with a bias in favour of conduct. This has had an especial influence upon the study of social subjects and particularly of history, and is the main reason for the backward state of the science of history, because the historian is prevented by political and moral considerations from following the rules of a strictly scientific investigation.

CHAPTER II

THE OBJECT OF HISTORY 12

There is much controversy as to what the object of history should be. But among the many diverse opinions there is one object which has never been clearly stated. A proper study of history will help to teach man his relation to the universe. A study of history is also, of course, necessary for the improvement of the art of government ; but as at present conducted it is largely useless for that purpose, since the desire to communicate political and moral instruction prevents proper scientific investigation. The course which the so-called science of sociology has pursued is a conspicuous instance of this truth. The scientific principles proffered by many writers, such as Lord Morley, are inconsistent with the method which they actually pursue in historical investigation. The ordinary procedure of observation, hypothesis and verification must be imported into history before it can become really scientific. In particular the subjects of government, war and of the causes of national success require to be studied in this way.

v

vi   HISTORY AS A SCIENCE

PAGE

CHAPTER III

GOVERNMENT AND THE INDUCTIVE STUDY OF HISTORY . 38

Though much has been written upon government, the subject has never been treated in a strictly scientific way. The educational method of inculcating principles rather than the inductive method of observing facts has been followed. Historians for instance have, as far as possible, averted their eyes from the phenomena of absolute government which, on the inductive method, should be regarded as of the utmost importance. The intrusion of metaphysical ideas into history is particularly to be deplored, since it causes the observation of facts to be regarded as an entirely subordinate consideration. Moral philosophy also exercises a prejudicial influence by disparaging government and denouncing its need as a confession of moral failure. Constitutional historians are also engaged upon purely educational, not scientific, ends, and have caused exaggerated attention to be paid to the doings of " political assemblies " which are credited with achievements and powers which do not belong to them.

CHAPTER IV

WAR AND THE INDUCTIVE STUDY OF HISTORY   .   . 56

Owing to reasons already laid down, the subject of war has never been properly discussed. Nevertheless, its inveteracy marks it as a phenomenon of the deepest scientific interest. It is the result of psychological causes beyond the reach of the individual, since bodies of men (nations) commit acts from which they would shrink as individuals. The only practicable method of terminating war is by a coalition of those nations who are satisfied with their present position, though the League of Nations may do useful preparatory work. With regard to the Great War, the English insufficiently realized in the beginning that it was not a war between France and Germany, but between Germany and the world, for which they should have prepared long beforehand. For the same reason it was the duty of the Americans to have intervened long before they did. The claim of the Americans to a superior international morality cannot be admitted. Though their selfish defalcation constitutes a setback to the peace movement, there is no reason to despair if due regard is taken of the psychological peculiarities of nations.

CHAPTER V

REVOLUTION AND THE INDUCTIVE STUDY OF HISTORY . 82

Mrs. Webster, by an unemotional re-examination of the facts of the French Revolution, has given us a notable example of the inductive study of history, rejecting the usual educational method, which seeks to show that Revolu-

CONTENTS

PAGE

tion is merely a righteous punishment for misgovernment. The fact that Mrs. Webster's view of the cause of this revolution is weak does not in any way impair the main value of her investigation. Such a work has a political as well as a historical interest : especially at the present time when the scientific study of revolution is above all things necessary. Revolutionary excesses are the result of the abolition of a political control in the first place ; and of a certain mental perversion in the second. Revolution gathers its fatal momentum because rulers are initially ignorant of its real nature. It is never recognized that one of the main defects of the French government, and one of the main causes of the French Revolution, was the denial of the free career to political talent. Revolution can always be prevented or defeated by a timely resolve on the part of the law-abiding majority to come forward in defence of the constitution and of themselves, and this is a lesson which the English have now learned.

CHAPTER VI

The Study of History from the Point of View of Conduct III

History, which in the preceding pages has been regarded from the point of view of science, must now be regarded from the point of view of conduct. The art and science of politics must be kept distinct. Machiavelli has been condemned to obloquy because he found from a strictly inductive study of history that anarchy can only be cured by the forcible imposition of a strong central government, and advised Lorenzo accordingly. Morley's criticism is altogether uncomprehending and unjust. The case of Machiavelli shows clearly the limitations which are set to the use of the inductive method in history. Parallel between Bismarck and Machiavelli. The "real-politik" of the Germans which led to the war of 1914 was derived from an inductive study of history. Though the teaching of history cannot be closely followed, it cannot, on the other hand, be disregarded as Liberals, Radicals and Socialists believe. The differing requirements of knowledge and conduct are as striking in the sphere of economics as in the sphere of politics. The study of political economy has been relatively successful because it was coldly scientific. But the disregard of humane considerations which this treatment involved was rightly denounced when carried into real life, and was followed by the rise of socialism as a protest. Socialism is a tendency which is useful only if confronted by a strong opposition, and will benefit not by securing its own demands but by modifying the attitude of its opponents. Concluding remarks.

Index 135

" The ideas which are to transform the study of history are lying unrecognized somewhere on the pages of the very text-books with which we have been familiar from childhood. To find a new meaning in old and well-established facts is the very essence of the scientific process."—From the introduction to *Government by Natural Selection.*

HISTORY AS A SCIENCE

CHAPTER I

THE INHERENT CAUSE OF FAILURE

AMONG the various considerations upon which the progress of the world has depended, two will generally be admitted to have had very great influence. One of these is the desire to promote knowledge, and the other the desire to improve conduct. The advancement of knowledge and the maintenance of a reasonable moral code have been throughout history the essential prerequisites of civilization. There would be nothing remarkable about the existence of these two tendencies were it not for the relation in which they stand to one another. It might have been anticipated that those who desire to do what they can for the furtherance of the highest interests of mankind would devote themselves amicably whether to the mental or moral improvement of their fellow-creatures. The truth is, however, that there seems to be an actual incompatibility so far as the generality of the human race is concerned between the simultaneous promotion of these two objects. Knowledge and conduct, instead of being firm allies throughout the history of social evolution, as might have been expected, have been found to a large extent in open conflict.

Nor is this all. The interest excited by this curious phase of conflicting tendencies in social evolution is by no means exhausted by the statement of its actual

HISTORY AS A SCIENCE

existence.   The mode of its operation is equally important and closely concerns the argument of the present work. For it is remarkable that the contest has never been waged on level terms.   Up to a certain point it is true that the interests of knowledge and of conduct are found to be identical, increase of knowledge implying improvement of conduct.   Presently, however, it comes about that men are forbidden to devote themselves with equal earnestness to these two aims, and the reason for this is that at a certain stage of social development the progress of knowledge seems to threaten the foundation of religious belief upon which conduct is so largely based ; and conduct, as a consequence, takes alarm and openly opposes the advance of knowledge except under conditions determined by itself.   It is unnecessary for the writer to pursue this argument further, since a chapter has been devoted to the subject in a previous work.[1]   It will be enough for the present purpose to discuss the matter only at such length as will serve to show its bearing upon the subject of the present volume.

Of this opposition a single recent but conspicuous instance may be given.   When, during the nineteenth century, those engaged on geology, sociology and anthropology arrived at conclusions which were inconsistent with the cosmogony of the Bible, they were unsparingly denounced by the majority of their contemporaries for publishing views calculated to unsettle religious belief, and consequently to undermine the foundations of conduct.   On the other hand, a resolute determination to enlarge the boundaries of science prevented men like Darwin and Huxley from allowing such considerations in any way to derogate from the right of free inquiry. This tendency to take divergent views as to the relative importance of knowledge and conduct is common in varying degrees to all the human race.   To such an extent is this true that individuals may be classified according

[1] See *Conditions of National Success*, Chapter II.

THE INHERENT CAUSE OF FAILURE 3

as they incline to one side or the other in this age-long controversy. Not only will a cursory examination of the works of well-known writers show definitely upon which side their preference lies, but a few moments of conversation directed to this purpose with any person of average intelligence would enable the curious to arrive at a similar conclusion. Moreover, this divergence of interest will be found to distinguish different nations and different epochs as well as different individuals. The Romans and Spartans, for instance, assigned the greater importance to conduct, and the Athenians to knowledge ; while in the England of the nineteenth century, though the Victorians made notable contributions to all branches of Science, the interests of conduct were clearly held to be of the greater importance by the nation as a whole ; so much so, indeed, that the affectation of superiority which the men of the present generation have seen fit to assume rests solely on the fact that they have had the courage to break down the barriers in the way of the extension of knowledge which hampered their mighty predecessors.

But though we have said that men may be divided into opposing parties in this matter, the numerical strength on either side has by no means been the same. Those who range themselves on the side of conduct have always been in a majority and have in consequence been able to a very large extent to impose their will upon the community, discouraging the kind of knowledge not approved by themselves, and rejecting discoveries which are unpalatable from the orthodox religious standpoint. In all ages and in all countries there is observable a tendency on the part of the majority to arrest the progress of knowledge at a point where it seems to the religious members of the community to be becoming dangerous. Knowledge has in consequence been unable to profit to the full extent by the devoted eagerness and self-sacrifice of its followers, who might by this time have carried discovery to un-

HISTORY AS A SCIENCE

imagined heights had they been permitted to utilize their full powers.

For a phenomenon so universal there must clearly be an evolutional sanction ; and this sanction is to be found in the fact that great as are the interests of knowledge, the interests of conduct are more important to the human race. Evolutionally speaking, the possibility of any systematic development of knowledge is dependent upon the previous existence of a well-ordered society. But the existence of a well-ordered society is impossible without a well-defined and carefully protected code of conduct. As things are constituted it is a necessary condition of progress that the cause of conduct should have a stronger following than the cause of knowledge, good principles being more essential than wide learning for the maintenance of social existence.

Since men must live before they can know, they are by nature more deeply concerned in protecting the foundations of morality than in extending the range of knowledge. It follows that wherever the interests of these two departments of life come into conflict, it is knowledge that must give way. The social organism is, in fact, so constituted as to assimilate with readiness the teaching or information which is good for conduct, while rejecting that which seems bad.[1]

There is, however, a further point of great importance to the argument of the present work. Hitherto this conflict has been spoken of as taking place between different parties. It may, however, be and very frequently is reproduced in the mind of one and the same

[1] That this should be so is in strict accordance with one of the main facts upon which modern philosophy insists, that life is only possible because our senses are selective. This selection " is effected by the organism responding apparently to what is a necessity of its own existence " (H. Wildon Carr). We see and hear and are intellectually conscious of not all that is to be seen or heard or apprehended, but only so much as is consistent with the maintenance of a healthy and vigorous life.

THE INHERENT CAUSE OF FAILURE 5

person. It may so happen, for instance, that an individual may be endowed with strong religious convictions while at the same time he is keenly interested in the general progress of Science. Under these circumstances he will be fortunate if he is not one day assailed with terrible doubts or compelled to the sorrowful abandonment of one or other of his conflicting beliefs. There are many, of course, who are hardly conscious of any such opposition and who manage to convince themselves that their love of knowledge is as great as their attachment to established religion and can be reconciled with it. As a great thinker in the nineteenth century put it : " They shut the door of their laboratory before entering their oratory." But great as is the capacity of the human mind for self-deception it is sometimes found unequal to this task ; and in many a quiet country parsonage a silent tragedy has been enacted when the discovery has been made that the activities of an all-inquiring mind are forbidden to the follower of a definite creed. Until a religion is discovered which will remain undisturbed by any discoveries of Science such unhappy mental conflicts will always be liable to occur.[1]

The opposition in the mind of the individual between the claims of knowledge and of conduct is specially marked when social subjects are under discussion. Observation reveals that in those studies which are more immediately concerned with human life, in sociology for instance and in history, the generality of mankind are under an instinctive predisposition to take that view of the facts which seems most consistent with ethical standards. Though

---

[1] The celebrated naturalist, Canon H. B. Tristram, found himself involved in a predicament of this sort with regard to Darwin's *Origin of Species*. In obedience to his instincts as a naturalist he wrote to *The Times* on the publication of this work to say that Darwin's views were fully confirmed by his own observations. But when the subsequent publication of *The Descent of Man* revealed the logical consequences of this admission, he publicly withdrew all that he had previously stated.

6 HISTORY AS A SCIENCE

a few will always be found ready to face facts as they are, the vast majority are insensibly led to give them an aspect such as in their opinion will be conducive to the moral welfare of mankind, and they are continually being diverted from the pursuit of the actual truth by this over-mastering desire. The data of social science are also elements or facts of conduct, and the inquirer, reproducing in his own person the evolutional bias in favour of conduct, becomes incapable of dealing with his subject in a properly scientific way. In his mind is continually present the unacknowledged question : " What will be the effect upon morality of the opinion which I give to the world ? " And the opinion, in consequence, tends to be formed not in the way which is most consistent with the evidence, but in the way which seems likely to produce the most beneficial social consequences.

It is the object of the present work to show that the unsatisfactory state of the study of history is largely due to the conflict in the mind of the historian between the interests of conduct and the interests of knowledge, which has just been described.

We are sometimes told that the complexity of history is so great and the causes at work so infinite that its reduction to scientific order is a task beyond the capacity of man. This excuse might be worth entertaining if scientific treatment had ever really been applied. It is the object of a science to investigate a given set of phe-nomena in order to discover the principles in accordance with which they take place, the laws of co-existence and succession as they are called. In order to obtain this result two most important conditions must be secured. There must be in the first place accuracy of observation ; and in the second place freedom to form, in accordance with evidence, hypotheses to account for the aspect which the phenomena assume, or, as in history, the course which events take. Only by following these rules can the indi-vidual discover new truths in whatever department of

THE INHERENT CAUSE OF FAILURE

science he happens to be engaged, or obtain that fresh light upon the workings of nature which we call the advancement of knowledge. Neither of these rules has been followed in the study of history. Though historians have from the first been actively occupied in the collection of data, yet, paradoxical as it may seem, they have not succeeded in combining this duty with a capacity for the observation of facts. The historian is a man whose house is divided against itself. As an investigator of social phenomena, who makes his fellow-creatures the subject of his study, he is compelled to recognize a double allegiance—to morals and to knowledge. While his desire to promote knowledge has prompted one course, his desire to forward morality has prompted another, to the detriment of strictly scientific procedure. It is well known that the significance of evidence varies with the emotional condition of the observer, and the majority of historians have approached their task in a frame of mind which has rendered them liable to see only what they wish to see, or even what is not there at all, and to import into the interpretation of events considerations which exist only in their own minds. The consequence is that historians have an inadequate conception of their duty as dispassionate observers of the actual process of political evolution. If a favourite political theory seems to be endangered by the admission of certain facts or tendencies, these facts or tendencies are liable to be ignored, and there is frequently a deliberate refusal to draw the natural inferences ; and, worst of all from the scientific point of view, there may be an inclination to tamper with the data in order to arrive at a desired conclusion.

In the next place, the second requirement of a progressive science, freedom to form hypotheses based upon the evidence before him, has been almost entirely forbidden to the historian. In history, as in other sciences, there are certain phenomena which stand out in such a way as to suggest that they are of permanent importance, and

8 HISTORY AS A SCIENCE

which, if used as the basis of a provisional hypothesis, might be capable of throwing a valuable light upon the process of social evolution. As will be pointed out in the course of the present work, war and absolute government are such phenomena, and it is upon the accurate and unbiased investigation of these and similar questions that the very possibility of a science of history depends. Upon these, therefore, the free play of a scientific imagination should be permitted. Yet, as will be more fully shown in the final chapter of the present work, these are the very questions upon which freedom of speculation is forbidden, since it has been already laid down by moralists and political doctrinaires how the historian shall treat them and what he shall think about them. The rules which he must obey are not the rules of scientific investigation but the rules which support social morality and political idealism. Though these events are his data, though they fall within the category of " observed phenomena," he may not form hypotheses about them in the true scientific manner, but must treat them in the way prescribed by those who have the interests of conduct rather than the interests of knowledge at heart. It is no wonder then that historical science, being prevented from observing with the required accuracy, and from following hypotheses with the required freedom, being cut off, that is to say, from the two main sources of vitality, should have languished in sterility, and should have failed to obtain results proportionate to the wealth of material at its disposal and the genius and industry of the workers engaged. It is no wonder that history, though it has somewhat extended its scope, remains in practically the same condition as it was in the time of Thucydides.

It may have been wise in the past that mankind should be treated like children from whom the real truths of life are deliberately concealed, but a stage of social evolution has now been reached when the disadvantages of this process are greater than the gain. The cause of

THE INHERENT CAUSE OF FAILURE 9

civilization is intimately bound up with that ascertainment of truth upon which the advance of science depends ; and if there is in the minds of those who are supposed to be engaged upon historical research a continual tendency to evade the truth in the interests or supposed interests of morality, it is quite certain that the study upon which they are engaged will not make adequate progress. This will be clear if we compare the use which historians on the one hand and the leaders of science on the other have made of their opportunities.

History is a subject which makes an almost universal appeal to the world in general. It forms a leading feature of the educational system of every civilized country, while for the typical thinker the life story of humanity constitutes a problem of never-ceasing interest. This can be said of no other subject, not even mathematics. Accordingly, with its double appeal to the sympathies of the highest and the lowest in the intellectual scale, it might have been supposed that the interest so caused would have stimulated a progress greater than that made in any other study. This reasonable anticipation is very far from having been realized. The determination to leave no corner of life and nature unexplored which has inspired the marvellous advance of other sciences has had no such effect on history. With a handicap in its favour which ought seemingly to have ensured its being first, history is actually last. If history is to occupy the position to which by its importance it is entitled, it can only be by effecting a reform of method upon the lines already indicated.

If, however, such a reform is to come about, it would seem from the circumstances of the case that it is not likely to be initiated by historians themselves, but must, as it were, be forced on them from outside. Historians, without actually publishing any " Articles of Association," have formed themselves into a sort of guild or corporation, bound by the moral conventions described,

HISTORY AS A SCIENCE

and few have ventured to disregard them. Moreover, knowing that they are engaged in the pursuit of a study of which the record goes back for more than two thousand years, during which times some of the greatest names in the intellectual history of the world have been numbered among them, they are full of the greatest admiration for their profession and for one another, and find it difficult to believe that all that is possible in history has not been already achieved.[1] If the paralysing weight of convention and tradition is to be removed, it has long been apparent that the initial steps must be taken by someone who is free from this somewhat inordinate respect for historians and their methods. It is for these reasons that the present writer, who can make no claim whatever to be regarded as a historian, ventures to come forward as a critic of methods which have for so long been in general and unquestioned use.

To sum up—the view which will be supported in these pages is as follows: The reason why the talent and industry displayed in historical study in the past has been condemned to comparative sterility is to be found in the fact that the study of history has been affected by the conflict between knowledge and conduct. Historical events, in so far as they form the data of a positive science, fall under the department of knowledge; but since they are at the same time the acts of human beings they belong also to the department of morality or conduct. While other inquirers have been able to devote themselves in singleness of purpose to the duty of accurate investigation alone, historians have been distracted by the double appeal to which they are subjected. The student of physics or chemistry is capable of observing facts in a detached impartial manner, standing outside his phenomena, so to speak, and being from the emotional point of view entirely indifferent to the nature of the

[1] As will be shown later, this attitude is particularly noticeable in the case of G. P. Gooch.

THE INHERENT CAUSE OF FAILURE 11

discoveries he may make or the conclusions he may draw. The laws of chemical or other change which may be revealed have no significance except in so far as they may enlarge the range of his knowledge. However different the result may be from that which he anticipated, however little he may have expected the molecular combinations and attractions and repulsions which confront him, he is quite undisturbed. He is free to accept whatever truths his investigations may disclose, his sole duty being to observe with accuracy, and to suggest, with due subservience to the facts before him, some theory which may serve to explain what they mean and how they come to be what they are.

Not so with the historian. The cold impartial detachment of the man of science is not for him. Where the chemist and physicist can investigate the truth undeterred by any anxious regard for the effect of his discoveries upon conduct, he finds it impossible to be indifferent to the nature of the phenomena which he examines or the character of the conclusion at which he may arrive. *Homo est: humani nihil a se alienum putat:* and it is this sympathy, most excellent and praiseworthy from the moral and humanitarian point of view, which has made him a special pleader who is determined to find evidence in favour of certain moral or political ideals, and who insensibly gives that colour to his narrative which will invest it with the required significance. If human history is to succeed in formulating laws which will serve to explain the process of social and political evolution, it is impossible to acquiesce any longer in a system which is the negation of scientific method. The requirements of progress demand that history should be free from the restraints hitherto imposed. The human race must be considered to have " attained its majority " and to be capable of facing the truth.

CHAPTER II

THE OBJECT OF HISTORY

THE question as to what form history should assume has been the subject of ceaseless controversy. A short examination of some of the various points put forward at different times will serve to show that the failure to agree on this point is due to the absence of any clear conception of the object at which history should aim. There is first of all the idea, ridiculed by Seeley, that history is merely a branch of literature—which would reduce the question practically to one of style. In the next place, granting that a historian must have a serious object, should he be content to elevate the intellectual tastes of his readers by lending an unwonted charm to otherwise uninteresting topics? Should he merely attempt to beguile them into more serious studies by making history more attractive than the latest novel? Should he have no higher object than to write in such a way "*ut vera fictis libentius legantur*," as the inscription on Macaulay's monument at Cambridge suggests? The desire to raise the standard of public taste in anything is laudable, but it is not, strictly speaking, a historical object. Too great attention to style even has its dangers. Frederic Harrison, for instance, is of opinion that "brilliant and ingenious writing has been the bane of History: it has degraded its purpose and perverted many of its uses."[1] On the other hand, it is certain that history loses nothing by being made bright and attractive, provided this idea is subordinate to a more

[1] *Meaning of History*, p. 8.

THE OBJECT OF HISTORY 13

serious purpose. If a further and more important object is kept in mind, no fault can be found with the historian for expressing his views with the greatest lucidity he can command, or for deepening by his literary skill the interest of his readers in the great drama of national existence. And if by these means he is able to beguile any considerable portion of the public into adopting as a recreation a study not usually so regarded, this is so much to the good. It is clear, however, that though history gains by being made presentable, there is a point beyond which the indulgence of the artistic spirit is irrelevant. Though Birrell eloquently deplored the "dethronement of Clio by scientific writers like Seeley," obviously the study of history must be regarded as something more than an opportunity for popular entertainment or literary display.

Dr. G. P. Gooch, in his *History and Historians*, tells us of the existence of a Prussian school, an Oxford school, a romantic school, a political school and a fatalistic school of history. It is a relief to be able to counter this bewildering variety of opinions by Professor Bury's downright statement that "history is a science neither more nor less," and, with him, to look forward to the time when "there will no longer be diverse schools of history but a single science." Not only, however, is there a difference of opinion as to the general attitude to be adopted towards history : there is a further difference of opinion as to whether it should be studied as a whole or in parts. Should history be written in periods, or are the subjects it deals with so interconnected as to make it irrational to study history otherwise than in its entirety? Polybius is of opinion that those who study history in distinct portions which have no relation to one another, and who expect thereby to get a knowledge of the whole, are like a man who hopes from the fragment of a dismantled body to realize its strength and comeliness when alive. Similarly, Ranke gives it as his

HISTORY AS A SCIENCE

opinion that "no history can be written but universal history." "The central doctrine of Freeman's works was the unity of History. . . . Yet Stubbs devoted a considerable part of one of his lectures to an attack on his friend's philosophy. Classical, mediaeval and modern history, he said, could be usefully studied apart. In the world of action there was continuity; but in the world of thought and feeling, about which Freeman knew little and cared less, there were deep gulfs." [1]

Yet though the causal interconnection of history from beginning to end is undeniable, it will be argued later that the detailed study not only of particular nations but of national institutions, such as government, and of national habits, such as war and revolution, is essential for that kind of history which concerns itself with the principles of political and social development and the causes of human progress.

The truth is that these and other difficulties and points of disagreement will disappear, or will be reduced to comparative unimportance, when once the question is decided as to the place of history among the other subjects of human knowledge. History is a portion of knowledge. Clearly then, before we have decided upon the proper method of history, we must be prepared to deal with the question of knowledge as a whole, and must endeavour to explain what is the great work which it performs for the human race.

It is generally assumed that the functions of knowledge are of two kinds only; first, to train and develop the capabilities of the individual; and secondly, by discovering the secrets of nature to increase the power of man over his environment. But, important as these two objects of knowledge are, there is another more important still, and that is to teach man his relation to the universe. The interest of this final object must in the end transcend that of the other two.

[1] Gooch's *History and Historians,* p. 351.

THE OBJECT OF HISTORY 15

Philosophy, in spite of all its efforts, has so far failed to penetrate the mystery of life. Man must be regarded as a creature working in the dark. We neither know whence we came, whither we are going, nor why we are here. From the scientific point of view the only source of possible illumination is knowledge gained from experience. By amassing all available information on every conceivable subject, man may eventually be enabled to divine the purpose of his existence. At least these are the only lines upon which success can be expected, unless sources of supra-normal revelation are opened up. Failing that, we are thrown back upon the human intellect and its power of interpreting phenomena as the only reliable authority. Very slowly through the ages knowledge of all kinds has been accumulating, and there is no single branch of it which does not bear at least indirectly upon the question of the origin and destiny of man. Each single science makes its contribution to this grand total. All the information gained about the nature of the world in which we live is indirectly information gained concerning our relation to the universe, and will eventually help to throw light upon the part we play in it. And of all these branches of investigation none surely can be more important than history, the inquiry which deals directly with the actions of man, and investigates the laws of human development.

From time to time great religious teachers have arisen who have either claimed or have been credited by subsequent ages with possessing a knowledge of the reason of man's existence. But the account which they give is so obviously the product of the credulous and unscientific times in which they lived, and is in addition so frankly educational, so obviously inspired not by a desire for an accurate study of facts, but by the wish to be morally helpful, in accordance with the tendency described in the previous chapter, that it cannot stand the scrutiny of an enlightened age. Already more than half the intelligent

HISTORY AS A SCIENCE

classes regard the interpretation of the universe given by various religions as belonging to the region of pure fable, though they are ready to accept scientific proof of an evolutional purpose behind them. Some day the whole of the intelligent classes will do the same, and they will be speedily followed by those incapable of forming a judgment of their own. Under these circumstances the need of replacing these mythological guesses at truth by some fuller comprehension will become more and more apparent. Scientifically speaking, there is no other means of effecting this object than by inductive observation of the nature of the world in which we live, and the forces by which we are surrounded ; and history is, or should be, the final study in this investigation. The history of human evolution in its various aspects, political, social and economic ; the phenomenon of progress and its causes ; in a word, the process by which the leading nations have arrived at their present state of civilization : when all these subjects have been investigated on strict scientific principles we shall at least be brought nearer to a comprehension of the meaning of life than is possible in any other way. The study of history, that is to say the life story of humanity, is the culmination of tendencies which are observable in the whole previous course of science.

Of the other two purposes which history as a part of knowledge subserves, that which relates to the education of the individual and the enrichment of his character need not detain us here ; since the mental distortion caused by seeking to make history an educational force forms the main theme of the present work. Finally, therefore, we come to that function of knowledge which has the most direct utility, the increase of man's power over natural forces. Here it might at first sight be thought that history has little or no value, but this would be a profound error. It will, in fact, be found that, contrary to the general belief, the part played by history

THE OBJECT OF HISTORY 17

from this point of view may become even more important than the part played by any other science.

The material triumphs of civilization, as is well known, are due to the knowledge of natural processes which has given to man an increased ability to minister to his own wants. By this means he is enabled to modify his environment for the purpose of securing his greater happiness. But it is not generally perceived that if man is to complete that control over natural processes which physical science has commenced, he must carry his investigations into those departments of life with which, as a human being, he is more intimately concerned. The inductive study of history is the means by which this object can best be effected, for only thus can an insight be obtained into the method by which nature works in the domain of political and social evolution. The knowledge so obtained will be of infinite use to him in social reform, and will enable him to set about his task in a really intelligent manner when he attempts to introduce into his economic and political environment those changes which are necessary for future progress.

According to the present theory, although the social and political evolution of the human race takes place up to a certain point unaided by the conscious efforts of the individual, the human intellect is presently brought into play as the final and decisive agency in the process of human development. There are therefore two possible issues with which humanity is confronted. If the necessary progress is made in the discovery of the laws of political and social evolution, the advent of the relatively ideal conditions of life to which we may reasonably look forward will be materially accelerated. If, on the contrary, we remain in our present ignorance of these laws, it is perfectly possible that the advent of these conditions will not only be indefinitely retarded but may even be prevented altogether.

It has always been the privilege of intelligent man to

HISTORY AS A SCIENCE

improve upon the conditions by which he finds himself surrounded. Human interference with the course of nature is, according to the present view, part of the course of nature. This truth applies to politics as well as to material conditions. Hitherto, however, in consequence of his ignorance of the process in which he was endeavouring to take part, the interference of man in politics has been too frequently ill-conceived, ill-timed and ill-applied. It is the function of a true science of history to remedy this defect, first by enabling us to learn what is the general course which political evolution has followed, and then by showing us in what manner the original process may be altered for the better.[1]

Perhaps it will be said that this is a task upon which historians have already been engaged from the time of Thucydides onward. This is true only to a limited extent. While to themselves historians seem to be engaged in accurate investigations after the true scientific manner, they have, as pointed out in the previous chapter, very little intention of taking into account uncongenial facts and tendencies, especially such as are inconsistent with certain popular theories of government and political conduct. Though occasional instances of this peculiarity have attracted the notice of critics, its almost universal prevalence has not been generally perceived. It has been said of Macaulay and Carlyle, for instance, that " while the English Whig employed history to justify his political convictions, the Scottish Calvinist used it to illustrate and reinforce his ethical teaching," as if such a disposition was something peculiar to these two. No doubt they display the educational or propagandist bias in a more easily recognizable form. But it is nevertheless a characteristic which from the very nature of the case is common in varying degrees to most, except Thucydides,

[1] Peculiar difficulties, it is true, attend the business of putting history to political uses—these will be fully discussed in the final chapter.

THE OBJECT OF HISTORY 19

who certainly wrote, as he says, for the instruction of posterity, but who instinctively knew that accurate observation was the best method of achieving his object.

A conspicuous illustration of this tendency is afforded in the works of Frederic Harrison. In one of his essays he asserts that " the true object of history is to show us the life of the human race in its fullness and to follow up the tale of its continuous and difficult evolution," [1] a sufficiently satisfactory definition, but one which has very little relation to his own practice. His work, like that of his master, Auguste Comte, was deprived of any real scientific value by the habit of attempting to convey valuable moral lessons and establish important scientific truths at one and the same moment. " Let this be our test of what history is and what it is not," he says, " that it teaches us something of the advance of human progress . . . that it shows us the nations of the earth woven together in one purpose, or is lit up with those great ideas and those great purposes which have kindled the conscience of mankind." Two distinct ideas are here treated as one. In the first place, it is stated that true history " teaches us something of the advance of human progress," a proposition to which no exception need be taken. In the next paragraph, however, we have a further and quite different suggestion, that in order to do this it must " show us the nations of the earth woven together in one purpose." This idea has nothing whatever in common with accurate observation. For if there is one thing more than another which the facts of history do not show us, it is " the nations of the earth woven together in one purpose." To the eyes of faith no doubt a movement in that direction may be discernible. We may even go further and hold the opinion that a general study of the principles of evolution warrants the presumption that a united humanity will be the outcome of the turmoil of the past. But to admit

[1] *Meaning of History*, p. 8.

HISTORY AS A SCIENCE

this is a very different thing to admitting that human progress has been due to unity of purpose among nations. There has never been any real unity of purpose among nations. On the contrary, they have from the first been engaged in ceaseless conflict, not only in time of war but even in time of peace, since commerce, which was supposed to bind them together, seems so far only to have increased their antagonism. Similarly, though the value of " those great ideas which have kindled the conscience of mankind " need not be underrated, it would be impossible to found a science of history if we should pay them the exclusive attention which the author recommends. The explanation of Frederic Harrison's remarkable view as to what constitutes proper history is, of course, as follows : Under the pretence of telling the historian how to approach his facts, he urges him to fix his attention chiefly or even entirely upon certain elevating tendencies, and with this end in view insinuates a panegyric on the beauty of human unity and the value of great ideas, entirely forgetting his professedly scientific object in the desire to administer a little useful exhortation. It is, in fact, deliberately implied without being actually stated that the proper method of unravelling the intricate causes of human progress is to fix our minds upon whatever in the past has been morally most encouraging. Here we have the educational motive in one of the most striking manifestations.

In a similar way Dr. G. P. Gooch informs us that " the key to the study of history is the unity of civilization." Though in appearance scientific, pronouncements such as these are in reality merely educational. It is true that the moral edification of mankind may best be served by emphasizing as much as possible whatever indications of unity can be discerned in history, but to suggest that such one-sided observation is the best method of unravelling the intricate causes of human progress is entirely untrue, and is as remote as anything can be from true

THE OBJECT OF HISTORY

scientific method. In the case of all such thinkers we have an example of the confusion which ensues when the attempt is made to pursue simultaneously a scientific and an educational aim, and to pretend to investigate causes while in reality aiming at the production of an impressive moral effect.

It is perfectly possible for historians to be vividly aware of the educational bias in others while surrendering to it themselves. Sismondi, for instance, complains of those who employ " history to establish the rights of kings and nobles, parliaments or people, instead of seeking for the causes of errors with a view to avoiding repetition." But when he himself starts with the *a priori* assumption that liberty is the true secret of national greatness, and directs his investigations with the avowed object of proving his point, when he asserts that " the absolute power of one or many is a poison " and " employs history to establish " these conditions, his procedure is practically identical. Inductive observation clearly proves that all such views on liberty require the most serious qualification before they can be regarded as even approximately true. As will be shown in the succeeding pages, this tendency of historians to deny the efficiency of any political methods except those which are in accordance with the constitutional ideas of the present day is a fatal obstacle to the inauguration of a proper science of history.

Again, while Thiers says that " to judge men fairly," meaning, as the context shows, to write history fairly, " we must extinguish all passion in our souls," nevertheless in his *French Revolution* and his *Consulate and Empire* the spirit of real scientific detachment is entirely wanting. J. R. Green's criticism is frankly educational when he praises Freeman's *Norman Conquest* because " it glows with a passionate love of civil freedom." To glow with a passionate love of any preconceived idea is not the state of mind which conduces to a scientific appreciation of the

HISTORY AS A SCIENCE

diverse phenomena of history. With regard to German historians, Mommsen it may be admitted comes very near the true inductive method; though he, together with some of the later German publicists, falls into an error which will be the subject of criticism in the chapter upon war and in the final chapter. Ranke's expressed intentions were quite correct. " I resolved," he says, " to avoid all invention and imagination in my work and to stick to facts." " The aim of my history is merely to show what actually occurred." Yet though this commendable resolution enabled him to escape the educational bias by declining " the task of judging the past and of instructing the present," he had a tendency which, as pointed out in the opening sentences of this chapter, if indulged too far is inconsistent with strict scientific investigation. According to Niebuhr, " he surveyed the past with the eyes not of a statesman but of an artist," a criticism which finds justification in his own confession, " It is so sweet to revel in the wealth of all the centuries, to meet all the heroes face to face, to live through everything again."

Dr. G. P. Gooch himself, from whom these quotations are mainly taken,[1] seems at times fully alive to the fact that the function of history is, as he says, " to discover the truth and interpret the movement of humanity." Yet, as already pointed out, his emphasis on the unity of civilization seems to show that his scientific perceptions are at the mercy of his educational proclivities. Again, while in his criticism of Froude he lays it down that " the main duty of the historian is neither eulogy nor invective, but interpretation of the complex processes and conflicting ideals which have built up the chequered life of humanity"; he tells us in the same chapter that good government " if maintained by the sword " is not worth having. Yet an unbiased reading of history would surely show us that government by force is an extremely valuable thing,

[1] *History and Historians*, pp. 329–39 and *passim*.

THE OBJECT OF HISTORY

when as frequently happens there is no alternative but anarchy. In the present writer's *Origin of Government* it is shown to be extremely doubtful whether civilization could have survived if " government by the sword " had not been enforced during the long intervals when constitutional government was not available. Among " the complex processes which have built up the chequered life of humanity " absolute government is, in fact, one of the most important. Dr. Gooch, though he implies on the very first page of his book that the ideal of history must be a " disinterested attempt to understand and explain the course of civilization," is disinclined, when it comes to the point, to adopt the procedure which he himself recommends.

But perhaps the best illustration of the unfortunate consequences which ensue from the attempt to combine moral instruction with scientific research is to be found in the rise and development of the very science which was inaugurated to remedy the shortcomings of history proper, the science of sociology. Though Comte, the famous founder of the study of sociology, deliberately placed before himself the idea of giving a really scientific account of the process of social evolution, he was quite unable to resist the bias which converts the investigator of historical facts into the ardent advocate of certain political or moral principles, and he abandoned after a certain time his scientific purpose of discovering truth for the more alluring prospect of being the moral and social regenerator of the human race. Overcome by sympathy for those human beings whom he should, strictly speaking, have regarded merely as the data or " subject " of his study, Comte relinquished the dispassionate investigation of social phenomena which a really scientific method would have enjoined. The impartial investigator of facts was presently transformed into the founder of " the religion of humanity."

The consequences which ensued are well known.

HISTORY AS A SCIENCE

Though the study of sociology was begun under brilliant auspices, it has proved as unproductive as the history it was meant to supersede, for exactly the same reasons and in consequence of exactly the same faults. Historians had contented themselves with mere narrative enlivened or perverted by their political prejudices. It was the object of sociology, on the other hand, to go much more systematically to work, and to investigate thoroughly the reasons why man had so signally failed to attain satisfactory social and political conditions during more than three thousand years of intelligent existence. From the moment, however, that the educational idea intervened, the execution of the original project became impossible ; the interests of conduct, as usual, began to assert the superior claim to attention, and the idea of the systematic study of the facts gave way to the idea of reforming mankind by " showing the nations of the earth woven together in one purpose or lit up with those great ideas and great purposes which have kindled the conscience of mankind." The cause of knowledge is not advanced when the philosopher leaves his proper business of inquiry for the premature application of imperfectly ascertained principles.

Of the resulting confusion a notable instance may be given. Sociologists took it for granted on the strength of some loose analogies that the method of the growth of a society or " social organism " was largely identical with the method of the growth of the individual human body. Sociological and biological processes, they said, took place in a similar way and on similar principles. In accordance with this presumption they proceeded to treat humanity itself as an organism of which nations were the component parts, and they met the obvious difficulty which the fact of incessant international hostility presents by the following remarkable piece of reasoning. Since humanity is an organism, harmonious co-operation between the nations or parts of which it is composed must

THE OBJECT OF HISTORY 25

obviously be more " natural " than antagonism. By the help of this *petitio principii* they were enabled triumphantly to arrive at the conclusion at which they had been aiming from the first, that war was something abnormal, something which perversely interfered with the true evolutionary process. Instead of forming their opinion as to the method of social evolution after inductive observation of the facts, they assumed on the strength of an imperfect biological analogy that they already knew that method, and they began to praise or blame the phenomena according as they agreed or not with this foregone conclusion. Sociologists could thus be seen in the act of abandoning the part of scientific observers in order to take up that of ethical teachers, encouraging certain tendencies by a flattering notice and discouraging others, more pronounced from the scientific point of view, by their condemnation.

Herbert Spencer himself was a peculiar adept at this question-begging method of procedure. Unable to deny that war has been an inseparable accompaniment of human evolution, and knowing that this was inconsistent with the belief in " humanity as an organism," he was in no way induced to modify his original conception, but turned instead to denunciation of mankind for ruining their own happiness and incidentally spoiling his theory by indulgence in so wicked a practice. It is in consequence of this almost childish procedure that the so-called science of sociology, though it has enunciated a few vague generalities, has proved to a large extent a barren and unproductive study. Because the educational desire to improve human nature was allowed to predominate over the scientific duty of observing facts and tendencies, neither of these objects has been attained. Mankind has not been reformed nor have the foundations of a proper science of history been laid.

Lord Morley also seems to have been aware in a subconscious sort of way that something was amiss in the

26   HISTORY AS A SCIENCE

treatment of history, and his troubled mind drove him to suggest inconsistent solutions of the difficulty at different times. Although in his essay upon Guicciardini he says : " After all, the vital question about a historian is whether he speaks the truth " ; later on in another essay in the same volume when he has again raised the question of fidelity to fact he asks " whether the historian is to present all the facts of his period or subject ? If he must select, how can he do it, how can he group, how can he fix the relation of facts to one another, how weigh their comparative importance without some sort of guiding principle, conception or preconception ? "[1] Conception, yes, but preconception, no ! The confusion of thought which prevails upon this subject could hardly be better demonstrated than by the way in which these two vitally distinct suggestions are here treated as if they were practically the same, or at least as literary variations of an equivalent idea. Though we must undoubtedly have some guiding principles or " conception " to enable us to estimate the importance of the data and to fix their relation to one another, this conception must be derived from a study of the facts before us and not imported from elsewhere. We immediately part company with scientific procedure if this guiding idea is a " preconception," derived from some other source than that of observed fact, because this must necessarily prevent the investigation from being conducted in the proper inductive way.

Elsewhere, indeed, when he has momentarily freed himself from his educational proclivities, Lord Morley shows himself to be perfectly aware of this truth. He evidently agrees with Turgot in the view " that to hold a theory otherwise than as inference from facts, is to have a strong motive for looking at the facts in a predetermined light (the ' preconception ' which Morley elsewhere recommends), or for ignoring them : an involun-

[1] *Morley's Miscellanies*, 4th series, p. 228.

THE OBJECT OF HISTORY 27

tary predisposition most fatal to the discovery of truth, which is nothing more than the conformity of our conception of facts to their adequately observed order."[1] We could not have a better account of the way in which an investigator should proceed, or a better description of the besetting sin of historians ; and that too from the pen of a writer who, as we shall see in the final chapter, has sinned as grievously as any in giving his verdict against the weight of evidence, and in allowing his philosophic " preconception " to determine his attitude towards the political phenomena which he finds before him.

It is plain, then, that the principle of selection to be used in a science of history, the theory which is to explain the facts and determine their arrangement, must be derived, like the principle of selection in any other science, from the facts themselves, not from any outside source. The historian must not go to biology like Comte and Spencer, or to moral philosophy like Lilley and Carlyle and Ruskin, or to metaphysics like Lord Acton or to the tenets of philosophical radicalism like Lord Morley, for his theory, but must extract it from the actual historical data before him. To say that the really vital question for a historian is whether he tells the truth is to evade the real problem. For he cannot tell the truth unless he first sees it ; and he cannot see the truth " if he has a strong motive for looking at the facts in a predetermined light." Unless he can avoid this " predisposition most fatal to the discovery of truth," the utmost industry in getting hold of " good documents " and " reliable authorities," which Morley at another time seems to think the one thing needful, will avail him nothing. However important this may be in itself, it is only what Dr. Gooch calls " the winning of raw material." History requires more than this. Documents may be as good and authorities as reliable as possible ; historians may relate occurrences with the most minute

[1] *Morley's Miscellanies*, Vol. II, p. 62.

HISTORY AS A SCIENCE

fidelity; their good faith may be beyond the possibility of question. But unless they approach their facts in the proper scientific spirit and subject them to the proper scientific treatment, they are omitting the most essential part of the process necessary to make history a science.

An investigator who wishes to discover truth should make his mind, as far as possible, like the *tabula rasa* of the old psychologists, and be prepared to register first impressions faithfully and on a clear surface. But the mind of the average historian, so far from being a *tabula rasa* is more like a palimpsest, thickly covered beneath the surface as well as upon it with ideas which effectually interfere with the reception of a true impression from the facts; ideas which, however valuable from another point of view, are utterly irrelevant for the purpose in question, the proper interpretation of the phenomena. Under the influence of the preconceptions with which he is plentifully equipped he is tempted to accept the slenderest proof in confirmation of views which for ethical or political reasons he is already determined to uphold. How, for instance, can a faithful estimate of the part played in social evolution by different types of government be made if the mind of the historian is permeated, like that of Lord Acton, with a deep sense of " the crime of civil and religious absolutisms." It is not in such a spirit or by such methods that other sciences have been built up and their triumphs achieved, but by unfettered observation and hypothesis. Free speculation on the causes of historical events, institutions and tendencies, undeterred by the fear of consequences, is the only method by which the foundation of a science of history can be laid.

Free speculation, however, on such subjects, has been forbidden because of its tendency to weaken those *a priori* principles of political conduct which are considered necessary for the advance of civilization. This would seem to be the reason why the energy of the

THE OBJECT OF HISTORY 29

historian, prevented from finding its proper outlet in the ordinary scientific way, has been driven to expend itself upon the incessant accumulation of data. This passion for fresh facts would be entirely commendable if it were regarded merely as the preliminary to the more important step of suggesting some unifying theory. Yet not only is this further step very seldom taken, but the opinion is hardly concealed that the historians who indulge in hypothesis are guilty of neglecting their proper business. The explanatory process which in the case of other sciences follows immediately upon the collection of an amount of data infinitely less than that in the possession of historians is not only withheld but actually discouraged.

Of this all-pervading tendency we have a typical instance in the works of a writer already mentioned, who, like Lord Morley, is unable to live up to his occasionally clear perception of what history should be. Though, as we have already seen, Dr. Gooch can give a satisfactory definition of the scope of history, yet in his general survey of the historians of the nineteenth century he manifests something very like hostility to any who are endeavouring to follow a more scientific line of procedure than that usually adopted. This hostility is apparent in his criticism of Seeley and of Mahan upon the value of whose contributions to the foundation of a science of history it is quite unnecessary for the present writer to insist. Amid some perfunctory expressions of admiration he insinuates the impression that Seeley's defects are greater than his merits. "Didactic history, however scientific in intention and stimulating in result, has its pitfalls." The works of Seeley are not in essence didactive. Though he certainly said : "history must have a relation to practical politics," he deliberately avoids the *a priori* attitude characteristic of educational historians, and contents himself with enunciating conclusions derived from a careful survey of the facts which he submits as

HISTORY AS A SCIENCE

it were to the judgment of the reader as he goes along. Again, though Dr. Gooch admits the quality of Seeley's work is high, this does not seem sufficient compensation for the fact that it was " slender in quantity." Apparently he did not make a sufficiently large contribution to the already overgrown mass of detail to entitle him to be ranked among the leading historians.

Mahan is another historian to whom we are indebted for an example of the brilliant results which the inductive method can be made to produce in the hands of a thinker of insight and originality. But the chief impression left on Dr. Gooch's mind seems to be a regret that " few new facts are brought to light." Here once more we have the belief implied that the chief duty of the historian is to collect materials but not to use them. With such critics the relation of the historian to his facts is that of the miser towards his hoard of gold, which he incessantly increases while shrinking in horror from the idea of putting it to any human use. What many historians apparently have yet to learn is that what is wanted is not to bring new facts to life but to utilize what we have already got, and it is the supreme merit of Seeley and Mahan that they have grasped this truth. Yet, to do as Mahan does, and as is done in other sciences, to treat old facts in such a way that they have a totally new and important meaning, and to show the determining influence which they have exerted on the history of the world, is to be merely a " brilliant amateur." [1] The more voluminous writers who are content to plod on in the old hopeless way are evidently more respected. In short, if approximation to any scientific method is of any value in history it is hard to resist the conclusion that Seeley and Mahan are excluded from the highest honours on account of their merits rather than their defects.

The use of hypothesis after the manner of the two writers just mentioned is essential for the progress of

[1] *History and Historians in the 19th Century*, pp. 373, 423, 485.

THE OBJECT OF HISTORY 31

history. If we ask what form that hypothesis should assume the answer is that, broadly speaking, the kind of theory to be adopted is a matter for the determination of each particular historian. The field of fact is to the philosopher or historical inquirer like the tract of country over which he hunts is to a dog, while hypothesis may be compared to the scent which the dog picks up. The dog and the philosopher follow up this scent to see what they can find. It may be a false scent, but in that case little harm is done ; they merely return and start out again in a fresh direction. One hypothesis, as we know, holds good until a better is found. This is the method of physical science and if it is copied history will become something more than " the imaginative guess at the most likely generalizations," which is all that Trevelyan allows it in the way of scientific achievement.

The characteristics of the leading nations of the world, together with the main features of civilization, are as we find them to-day the result of a certain definite process of development, the nature of which it is the business of history to disclose. It must discover the main principles in accordance with which social and political evolution has taken place. No new light can be thrown on this important problem by the old system of studying the history of a particular nation, and detailing the result in narrative form. More fruitful would seem to be the method of investigating separately certain institutions or phenomena which are common to the human race and which seem of decisive importance. It is the habit in other sciences to assume after a preliminary inspection of the facts that certain phenomena have exercised an influence transcending that of other phenomena in the matter under investigation, and these facts are then re-examined to see whether the hypothesis is correct. As has already been pointed out in the first chapter, the same procedure should be adopted in history. The most important point is that any such hypothesis should

HISTORY AS A SCIENCE

be derived not from some *a priori* principle of the mind, chosen on account of its educational value, but should be formed in accordance with the results of a strictly inductive observation.

Hardly less essential than the formation of the theory is the process of verification. Yet educational historians, who dispense with a properly formed hypothesis, have no need of such a process. The " preconceptions " in accordance with which they arrange their facts are above the need of verification. Verification is a procedure which applies to something uncertain, something speculative, not to the infallible principles with which the moralist or political philosopher is armed for investigation. In accordance with the unwritten precepts of the educational system historians are bound to assume that the tendencies which have had the greatest influence upon human progress are tendencies which the moralist or " advanced " political philosopher regards as especially beneficent. Their choice of hypotheses is thus unduly limited to agencies which have been deliberately designed to do good, or to tendencies which, morally speaking, may be expected to have that result ; and it follows that no other factor in civilization is looked for or even regarded as possible. Yet as a matter of fact the evidence which proves many of the causes of social and political advancement to have been non-moral, is very strong, so strong indeed as to be decisive according to scientific rules. Civilization could never have reached its present stage of development had it not been assisted by evolutional tendencies, which are neither moral, religious nor utilitarian.

While attempting in three preceding works to put into practice the principles of the inductive study of history, the present writer has found that while in other sciences the attitude of the public is already favourable to enterprise, in history the advocate of any new departure must create his own atmosphere. The present volume,

THE OBJECT OF HISTORY 33

therefore, which logically speaking should have preceded the others, has been written in order to explain what the theory of the inductive study of history implies in practice, to demonstrate if possible its necessity, to suggest the results that will certainly attend its systematic employment, and to insist on the futility of expecting any real progress so long as the old educational method remains in use. It will perhaps conduce to clearness if the reasons are now given for the mode of procedure adopted in the present and in the preceding volumes.

No one who approaches the study of history in the way usual in ordinary sciences, with the intention of selecting some central phenomenon to serve as a unifying conception, can doubt that government has exercised an influence upon the destinies of mankind which it is difficult to over-estimate. Yet though the whole fortunes of the human race since the first appearance of civilization have in one way or another depended upon government, and though it consequently offers a most tempting prospect to the intending investigator, it has never been studied in the purely scientific spirit which could alone reveal its nature and origin. There is no sufficient examination of the phenomenon of government as the expression, in the political sphere, of those evolutional tendencies which are concerned with the welfare of the social organism. It would seem to be essential for the comprehension of the part played by an institution like this that it should be studied apart from its connection with any particular nation. The isolation of important phenomena is as necessary in history as in other sciences.

In the next place the evolution of government, as we shall see in the succeeding chapter, so far as it has been separately treated, has been treated almost entirely from the educational standpoint; the desire, conscious or unconscious, to effect political improvement, has proved a disturbing influence in the way of a strictly scientific investigation. The study of the evolution of political

34 HISTORY AS A SCIENCE

control must be undertaken upon inductive principles if scientific results are to be attained. This the present writer has attempted to do in the works entitled *Origin of Government,* and *Government by Natural Selection.*

Closely connected with the subject of government are the phenomena of revolution and anarchy ; the adequate discussion of the one implies the discussion of the others. For this reason, and because it offers a conspicuous example of the determination of educational writers to pervert the plain meaning of facts in their endeavour to preach an impressive moral or political lesson, a special chapter has been devoted to the subject of revolution in the present work.

Again, with regard to the relation of societies to one another there is the same general objection to treating the subject in any but an educational manner. History studied inductively shows that war either actually or in prospect has been the rule and not the exception, and that it is a phenomenon of such importance as to require the most careful consideration. Consequently, although the educational theory forbids the entertainment of any such hypothesis on the ground that to recognize war as a natural process is to encourage it, the subject has been especially treated in this and in preceding volumes.

But if government and war have exercised a decisive influence upon the fortunes of the human race, they have done so intermediately through the influence which they have exercised upon the nation. The history of civilization is identified with the history of successful nations. The special object of the historian therefore is to discern the conditions of national success which, up to the present day, have been identical with the conditions of progress. The present writer has endeavoured to develop this idea in the work entitled *Conditions of National Success.* He has been blamed, perhaps with justice, for not giving an accurate definition of national success before attempting to throw light upon it. But the

THE OBJECT OF HISTORY

omission was deliberate since the opinion of the average man and of the average history as to which nations have been the most successful was quite sufficient for the writer's purpose. The thinker who can satisfactorily explain why the Greeks, the Romans, the French, the Germans, the Spanish, the Dutch, the British, have occupied the prominent position in history which they have occupied, and who can show why some of these nations have done better than others, will go a long way towards elucidating the causes of human progress.

In accordance with the requirements of the inductive method, these various questions have been approached from a purely scientific and even non-moral point of view. Is there then, it will be asked, no moral side to history ? Is this most human of studies to be reduced to a pitiless analysis of cause and effect, in which ethical considerations have no place ?   If the study of history is to be conducted on really scientific lines the inquirer cannot afford to spend his energies upon the wholly divergent undertaking of moral and political education.   Nevertheless, when the right of science to pursue its investigations in its own way has been granted, there still exists a moral side to the problem which cannot be overlooked.   It was pointed out in the opening chapter that the difficulties which beset the study of history arise from the fact that it was simultaneously concerned with the interests both of conduct and of knowledge.   After having dealt with history from the point of view of knowledge, it is therefore necessary to deal with it from the point of view of conduct, and this aspect of the question will be examined in the final chapter.

Meanwhile it is not without interest to speculate how the application of the inductive method is likely to affect the form which history, regarded as a subject of universal interest, has hitherto assumed.   Are the numerous readers to whom history is a kind of literary and intellectual entertainment with which they would not readily dis-

HISTORY AS A SCIENCE

pense, to be told that such indulgence is too unscientific to be any longer permitted ?

No such necessity is involved in the advent of a science of history. Though a dispassionate attitude is required of the accurate investigator, it is not everyone who will be content to regard the pathetic and moving story of humanity merely as so much material for the construction of a science of history. There will always be a large number who will demand a more human and sympathetic treatment of the accidents and sorrows, the hopes and tragedies of which history, from the dramatic point of view, consists. We are therefore forced to the conclusion that since there are two points of view from which history can be approached, the point of view of science and the point of view of conduct or sentiment, two kinds of history will be written to satisfy these varying requirements. There will be scientific history, the character of which has been sketched in the preceding pages, directed to the discovery of the principles of human evolution and the cause and nature of progress, together with the investigation of the national and other conditions which have been necessary to enable man to reach his present stage of civilization. On the other hand, there will be narrative history, which as an intellectual recreation must undertake to satisfy the eternal interest of man in the doings of his fellow-creatures. This will deal with the varying aspects of human fortunes, as revealed in the rise and fall of nations and in the moving spectacle of human greatness and human frailty playing their part in the great drama of national and individual existence. While the requirements of the human mind demand one kind of history, the requirements of the human heart demand another. Guedalla's instinct leads him aright when he claims that " there is a Muse no less than a method of history." If some writers insist on providing us with a cold unemotional analysis of events and tendencies, others will give us a vivid presentation of the

THE OBJECT OF HISTORY 37

fortunes of nations and individuals, instinct with sympathy and unobtrusively subserving, after the manner of the drama, the higher purposes of humanity. The story of the human race, of the martyrdom of man as one writer terms it, treated in a manner which makes a universal appeal to the human heart, has a charm which no amount of science can satisfy.

There is one kind of history, however, which will tend to disappear, the history which manipulates its facts in the endeavour to convey moral and political instruction. While brightly-written narrative history has a permanent value, educational history has none, and this truth seems curiously enough in the process of being illustrated in the case of a famous writer, Macaulay. His brilliant powers of narration still hold the attention of the world, while his political special pleading is being more and more disregarded. There were, in fact, two Macaulays, though he did not know it himself. The first was the Whig propagandist, the educational historian, who was compelled by the bias of his convictions to treat many of his facts almost, if not quite, dishonestly. The second was the dramatic narrator of historical events, with his unequalled power of making the dead past live once more. The first Macaulay is ephemeral, the second is a permanent possession. The one will soon be forgotten, because to falsify history, for however excellent a purpose, is an offence against moral principle as well as against scientific method. The other will remain, because to produce scenes from the life history of mankind in a vivid and touching manner is to make an enduring contribution to the higher pleasures of the world.

CHAPTER III

GOVERNMENT AND THE INDUCTIVE STUDY OF HISTORY

GOVERNMENT is the most important subject with which history has to deal. In a perfectly real sense the progress of the human race is identified with the evolution of government. It is therefore obviously a phenomenon about which we should have the fullest information possible. Unfortunately it is a subject so closely connected with the moral side of human relations that its study has been pervaded with a twofold measure of that educational spirit, which, as shown in the previous pages, is fatal to the use of the powers of observation. As the present writer has elsewhere shown, the object of constitutional historians has been the improvement of political conduct rather than the ascertainment of historical truth. We have had no really scientific investigation of the development of an institution, which history, if it is to make the most elementary claim to be regarded as a science, must examine without bias or prepossession of any kind. The most famous of all the treatises on Government, while preserving the outward appearance of an inquiry, is in reality a dissertation upon political ideals. " The end of government," says Locke, " is the good of mankind " ; and though he enunciates satisfactorily the object at which government ought to aim, his explanation of its origin is merely childish. It is not the motives which rulers ought to pursue, but the motives which they have actually pursued which must be studied if we are to discover the actual course which

38

GOVERNMENT AND THE STUDY OF HISTORY 39

nature has followed in the origin and development of a political control. A scientific statement of observed tendencies is what Locke and the educational writers never give us. As we shall see later, there are certain of these tendencies which the inductive study of history shows to have been intimately concerned with evolution of government. The influence which they have exercised upon human fortunes entitles them to the closest scientific attention. But because they are not altogether commendable from the moral point of view they pass unnoticed or are noticed only to be condemned as unworthy of serious examination. Men have not been so much concerned to discover how government comes to be what it is as how to make it what they wish it to be. This was the motive which inspired the famous social contract theory ; and though Morley and Acton and other famous writers are careful to show that they do not take such a theory seriously, they are themselves actuated in their governmental treatises by exactly the same spirit.

The duty of actual observation is ignored under the influence of a desire to make the facts subserve an educational object. For this purpose it is necessary to emphasize whatever constitutional aspects may be discerned in a government, and to ignore other aspects which are more prominent but which are less useful from the educational point of view. Locke and his numerous disciples see only what they wish to see, and will argue to the death rather than admit the significance of facts which might serve as an encouragement to undesirable political conduct.

To a mind unhampered by *a priori* views it might well seem that the evolution of government is a subject which might be investigated on inductive principles with the happiest results. When, however, it is antecedently laid down that only one kind of government, constitutional government, is worthy of attention such an inquiry is impossible.

D

HISTORY AS A SCIENCE

How very far such questions are from being decided upon inductive grounds, even by historians who are conspicuously free from any political bias, is shown by the famous judgment of Gibbon on the Antonines, whom he regarded as the only rulers who had endeavoured to perform their duties in the proper spirit. From the scientific point of view this is to form a conclusion, not from the vast bulk of the evidence, but from the single exception. Governments are divided into two classes, one of which consists only of the Antonines, while the other includes the rest of the rulers of the world. If the investigation were conducted upon scientific principles, it is the more numerous class which would merit attention. But where the object is to read a moral lecture to the rulers of the future, the niceties of scientific procedure are entirely out of place. From the educational point of view conformity to an ideal type, not frequency of occurrence, is the most interesting feature in a government ; on the other hand, governments which are most imperfect and which offend against every constitutional principle may have a far greater value for the scientific investigator than a government which arouses the admiration of philosophers. When, however, inquirers approach their subject with the determination to see no merit in any form of government which does not issue from the people, or is not sufficiently controlled by them, they are necessarily oblivious of the truth which inductive evidence reveals, that the authority of the vast majority of governments in history has not been delegated from below but imposed from above ; that they have, in fact, existed in virtue of a power which is derived from their own strength, and not from the voice of the people. This is a phenomenon which must form the starting-point of any scientific inquiry into the nature of government ; yet from the educational point of view it is the very last thing that can be admitted. The political philosopher, with his eye upon future developments, averts his gaze

GOVERNMENT AND THE STUDY OF HISTORY 41

from what he considers to be unpleasant and dangerous tendencies, and is concerned only to throw the weight of his recognition and approval on the side of that type of government which he has already upon *a priori* grounds judged to be best. The natural consequence is that the phenomenon of absolute government, which by its incessant repetition would for that very reason attract the attention of a really scientific observer, is not regarded by historians as being invested with any greater significance on that account. There is an overwhelming amount of evidence to show that the kind of government to which we owe the transition from savagery to civilization, was kept vigorous and efficient in early times by a process which ignores the very semblance of constitutional principles. Nothing can be clearer than the fact that what we call tyranny and usurpation have incessantly proved of the greatest benefit at certain stages of social development and at certain crises of national history. As the present writer has elsewhere pointed out, any prosperity which the Roman Empire enjoyed for a thousand years onward, from the time of Galba, was largely due to the resolute but unconstitutional action of some overmastering personality such as Vespasian or Constantine, which saved the world from the horrors of anarchy.[1] Historians of government are engaged not in investigating facts in the ordinary scientific sense, in order to form a theory from them : they are engaged in imposing a theory upon the facts. If the facts do not accord with the theory, so much the worse for the facts ; it is they and not theory which must give way. The result has been that the whole of the history of government is more or less deliberately falsified in order that confirmation may be found for the theories not derived, as they should be, from a study of the phenomena, but from some antecedent principles of the human mind. So long as the desire to influence political conduct is regarded as of more impor-

[1] *Origin of Government*, Chapter V.

HISTORY AS A SCIENCE

tance than the elucidation of historical truth, so long as there is a determination to discriminate against certain facts on ethical and *a priori* grounds, no real progress will be made in the scientific study of government.

Again, there are certain philosophers who, though they do not themselves write history, are determined to influence its treatment. They are the metaphysicians. The subject in which they are most deeply interested is the subject of liberty, and they have agreed to dictate to all who make a study of humanity what they consider to be the proper standpoint in the matter. In obedience to their suggestion the majority of historians have made liberty their idol, and have thereby rendered themselves incapable of giving due weight to any indications that the opposite principle may have been a useful and even an indispensable factor in the evolution of social and political existence. They reject, without examination, all the evidence which goes to show that the evolution of civilized man is a process which has frequently depended upon the suppression of liberty for considerable, even immense, periods. Still less are they likely to admit that the very capacity for the proper enjoyment of liberty is a product of the discipline which has been learned under its opposite strong, even tyrannical, government. They are, on the contrary, convinced that when liberty is granted all else follows as a matter of course ; that it has been practically the sole condition of human progress ; and that where it has been conceded civilization has advanced, where it has been denied civilization has been retarded. According to some, indeed, history is nothing else than a triumphant struggle for the possession of liberty, and the noblest task upon which the historian can be engaged is to prove this thesis. When we come to the chapter upon revolution it will be interesting to note how this mental prepossession has engendered a curious blindness to the elementary truth that the primary and most important function of all government is the

GOVERNMENT AND THE STUDY OF HISTORY 43

maintenance of law and order. We shall find in consequence a very general inability to understand all that the presence of political restraint ensures, and a disinclination to attribute to their proper source the horrors which may ensue when it is suddenly and unduly relaxed.

If we wish to discover the real relation of government to human life, all such ideas which determine beforehand our attitude towards the subject must be abandoned. The actual record of government in history must be studied in its entirety before deciding what its functions are. The historian's range of observation would thus be advantageously enlarged, and he would be free to notice many interesting features which he would otherwise have been compelled to ignore. If he should find government continually engaged in the extension of national power, in asserting its own prerogatives, and repressing movements dangerous to its authority to a much greater extent than in promoting the happiness of its subjects, he should not turn away with indignation, but should carefully consider these peculiarities with a view to deciding what light they throw upon the original functions of governments. Such activities should not be regarded as proofs of a deplorable aberration, but rather as indications that no satisfactory conclusions as to the nature of government could be formed which did not take them into account. Instead of holding that there was something the matter with the facts if they did not coincide with his theory, he would begin to suspect a theory which was not in accordance with the facts. The summary rejection of unpalatable data which is customary with the educational historian is forbidden to the scientific observer.

Surveying history as a whole, such an observer would not long be able to resist the conclusion that there was a good reason for most of these governmental practices which the educational historian condemns. It might, for instance, seem not improbable that the tendency to the

44 HISTORY AS A SCIENCE

establishment of arbitrary power upon which so much indignation has been expended is in reality an evolutional provision for assuring one of the earliest conditions of social existence, a strong political control. It might seem likewise that the desire to increase the power of the State rather than to foster its internal well-being, which is the cause of so much distress to humanitarians, is a provision of nature to meet the ever-present dangers of the international situation ; and that it is only when the government has been able to ensure the security of the community that it has ability or leisure to turn its attention to happiness of the individual. This is a consideration of which the importance will be more apparent when we come to the chapter upon war. In the never-ceasing turmoil of international existence it has been very difficult, even impossible, for rulers to be satisfied that they have attained security, and this it is which accounts for the comparative indifference with which, throughout history, they have regarded internal welfare. Most historians would assent to the conclusion that governments are to be valued in proportion to their success in assuring the possibility of individual self-development. Such governmental duties, however, come second and not first in the order of evolutional importance. Under certain rarely-attained conditions of national existence the individual has been able to insist upon determining to a certain extent his own course of life and thought. But even then, as is proved in the case of the Athenians and other nations, the attainment of this ideal is achieved at the cost of dangerous national insecurity. Inductive observation shows that the first and by far the most important function of government has been to ensure the safety of the community in war, and that to manifest exaggerated concern for the liberty of the individual is a certain method of ensuring defeat. Absolute power, instead of being a regrettable perversion of political authority, which no self-respecting people could bring itself to endure, is under

GOVERNMENT AND THE STUDY OF HISTORY 45

certain circumstances by no means only occurring in primitive times, the necessary condition of survival. All nations, we are told, get the government they deserve, by which it is implied that democratic government is an ideal which has always been within the power of a resolute people. It is difficult to say what any particular nation may deserve in the way of government, but what it actually gets is the type which is permitted by international conditions. The care which it is possible to spend upon the refinements of internal administration is in inverse ratio to the demands made upon government by the international situation.

Again, it is to the educational obsession that we must attribute the curious indifference manifested by political thinkers generally to the value of ability in government. The truth that the excellence of any performance must necessarily depend to a large extent upon the capacity of the performers is so obvious that we might naturally have expected historians to regard government by ability as one of the first conditions of national prosperity. It is not so regarded, however, and for the following reasons. The idea is of no value for educational purposes : the appearance of talent in the ranks of an administration cannot be ascribed to moral causes, nor its absence to the wickedness of anybody in particular. It comes and goes in obedience to no rule upon which a political dissertation for the advantage of future generations can be preached. It cannot be made greater or less by praise or blame ; above all, it has nothing to do with those engrossing subjects " liberty " and " the will of the people." The educational historian therefore looks upon it coldly as offering no opportunity for the exercise of his special functions. The educational theory is in fact based upon the assumption that government is not a matter of ability, but merely of good character and intentions, a view which had the support of Lord Morley, who dismissed the idea that intellect could make any difference by a contemp-

46 HISTORY AS A SCIENCE

tuous reference to " The new cant about efficiency." As we shall see later, it is Parliament upon which the eye of the historian is fixed, because Parliament alone is able to secure what is considered to be the only really important factor in government, dependence on the will of the people. And thus we arrive at the ridiculous position that so long as the people control the government, the capability of the government which the people control is of no consequence whatever. The result is that the presence of genius or talent in government has never been systematically encouraged as an essential element of national success. Such an attitude might have been disastrous in English history had it not been for the so-called principle of representation, which has had the unrecognized but infinitely valuable result of securing the admission of ability and even genius to the ranks of the administration.[1]

We have already seen how the metaphysical worship of liberty leads to a corresponding depreciation of the value of strong government. But there is also another important department of thought which lends encouragement to this unfortunate attitude of mind. Moral philosophy takes up the position that the need of government is merely a confession of human failure. One of the great objects of education is to make the principle of goodness self-supporting, and this object moral philosophy endeavours to achieve by instilling the conviction that real goodness is the outcome of voluntary effort alone. However excellent a device this may be for the purpose of strengthening the capacity for self-reliance, it implies a subtle disparagement and depreciation of government as an agency for good in human affairs. Goodness which results merely from fear of the law may be a contemptible thing to the moral philosopher, but nevertheless this method of producing goodness has been of inestimable value in the history of civilization. Having in mind the

[1] *Government by Natural Selection.*

GOVERNMENT AND THE STUDY OF HISTORY   47

horrible excesses which characterize periods of anarchy, it does not seem an exaggeration to say that the world as a whole owes from one-half to three-quarters of its morality to prohibitions and punishments, sanctions, as they are called, of one sort or another. The moralist, however, maintains that good conduct which is due to repressive influences is not morality at all, but merely an artificial state of mind and feeling, liable to vary with the strength or weakness of the source from which it arises, and at the mercy of any accident that may happen to the governing authority. All this may be perfectly true but does not in the slightest degree diminish the obligation under which civilization lies to the phenomenon of government.

But in advertising his contempt for a " morality which is created by Act of Parliament," that is to say which owes its existence to the presence of government, the moralist ignores a feature of the case which is of incalculable importance in the actual process of social evolution. Though government may not be able to create morality, it is the indispensable means whereby moral individuals are enabled to exist. Those who approve of the dictate of moral philosophy that men should be ready to die rather than to do wrong, are apt to overlook the devastating effect which, in the absence of government, such a principle would exercise upon society. It would leave the good at the mercy of the bad. The most important function of government from the social point of view, as the present writer has elsewhere shown,[1] is that it alters in the interests of progress the whole meaning of the struggle for existence, and tends to ensure the survival of a new kind of fittest, the intellectually and morally fittest, by saving them from the fate which they would otherwise meet at the hands of their superiors in brute strength. When moralists seek to lower the value of government on the ground that they want " to lead men to self-control,"

[1] *Origin of Government*, Chapter I.

48 HISTORY AS A SCIENCE

they are in danger of ignoring this most vital aspect of the problem. If the characteristics of a higher civilization are to be made permanent, and a nobler type of humanity is to emerge, it is necessary that sufficient numbers of good men and women should live in order to leave behind them like-minded descendants, and this transmission to future generations of the moral and intellectual qualities upon which civilization depends would be impossible without the protection of government. In short, in discussing moral progress it is impossible to leave out of sight the question of survival. Government imposes such conditions on the primitive struggle for existence that high moral qualities, which previously had no " survival value " but were on the contrary fatal to their possessor, are enabled to thrive and to exercise a humanizing influence which would otherwise have been unheeded. As we shall see later, the depreciation of government and the adoration of freedom from control entails a fearful nemesis in times of revolution.

But perhaps the perverse demeanour which is so generally adopted with regard to the subject of government reaches its climax in the case of the constitutional historian. This peculiarity, though treated in a previous work,[1] demands further mention in a chapter devoted to an examination of the causes which have prevented the scientific study of the history of government. Most historians, when they place upon events an agreeable interpretation which they will hardly bear, have done so under the influence of an impulse which they scarcely recognized. But to the department of history in question this partial excuse does not apply. Constitutional history is pursued with an apparently deliberate intention of falsifying the facts in order to force them into an agreement with the desired conclusion. The constitutional historian almost openly avows that the only view which

[1] *Origin of Government*, pp. 104–11.

GOVERNMENT AND THE STUDY OF HISTORY 49

he intends to hold is the one which suits his particular purpose. That purpose is the strengthening of the case for constitutional government by showing it to be founded on an array of precedents so formidable that no usurper or other evil person, who might contemplate dangerous innovations, would dare to carry his intentions into practice. He is determined to establish a view of the case which is useful rather than true. Human nature is such that one of the best methods of fixing a custom or habit is to prove or make a show of proving that it has always existed. The object in the present case being to stabilize the best possible rules of political procedure, it follows that it is in the highest degree advisable to prove that the rules in question have been consistently recognized from the beginning. The principle which political philosophers regard as of the highest importance is that government can exist only by consent of the governed. It becomes necessary therefore from the legal point of view for English historians to prove that in English history there has never been such a thing as government without the consent of parliament or people. Consequently in the case of any change of rulers, even if the ordinary man would seem to be warranted in regarding the affair as one of pure usurpation, it must be shown that it is the action of parliament, and not the ambition of a political adventurer, which has in reality been the decisive consideration.

Here we have the educational motive open and avowed, and the flagrant inconsistency between fact and theory is overlooked because it subserves a commendable purpose. The constitutional historian cannot produce the required conclusion without tampering with his data, and this offence against the most elementary principles of science is permitted because of the excellent educational results that are supposed to be achieved.

The reader will at once perceive that however useful this method of procedure may have been for ensuring the

50 HISTORY AS A SCIENCE

stability of the British Constitution, it renders impossible an accurate analysis of the origin and animating principles of government. No ascertainment of the actual facts is possible when the observer considers himself under an obligation to refuse all evidence that tends to show that the actual course of political evolution has not conformed to the requirements of high political theory. When the inquirer, in addition to systematic suppression of the truth, does not hesitate where necessary at the suggestion of actual falsehood, there is little chance of scientific result. To the outside observer, with no constitutional axe to grind, it is, of course, quite obvious that on more than one occasion the title to the English throne has been purely that of conquest. Usurpation, however, according to the English constitutional theory, does not exist ; and obviously we cannot decide upon the importance or unimportance of a phenomenon if, with the English constitutional historians, we deny that it has ever taken place.

As might have been anticipated, it has proved impossible to maintain this extraordinary attitude in the face of the growing scientific tendencies of the age. Just as it has been found necessary to abandon those portions of a religious creed which are in flagrant contradiction with the realities of science, so it has been deemed wiser by the most recent writers on the constitution to bring their conclusions into greater conformity with the actualities of history. The cause of real religion is not dangerously impaired by the abandonment of an impossible cosmogony, nor is the stability of the British constitution seriously threatened by the substitution of good history for bad. As the scientific tendency gains upon the educational the historian is freed from the fear that some malevolent political use may be made of his conclusion, and is encouraged to pursue his inquiries in a bolder spirit. Maitland, for instance, in boldly stating not only that there was such a thing as despotism in English

GOVERNMENT AND THE STUDY OF HISTORY 51

history, but that it actually had its uses, and saved the nation from a more terrible fate, makes an admission from which earlier constitutional historians would have shrunk in terror. " In fact we may regard Norman kings as despotic ; when there is not despotism there is anarchy : still a certain semblance of another form of government is maintained, government by a king who rules with the counsel and consent of his barons."[1] Whereas formerly we were told to believe that the actions of our rulers always took place upon proper constitutional lines, although they might occasionally wear the appearance of absolutism, we have now to be content if a certain " semblance " of governing with the counsel and consent of the barons is kept up. Similarly, none of the earlier writers would have dared to hint, much less to avow, that at certain points of English history it was necessary to choose between anarchy and despotism. Inductive observation, however, had its evidence been accepted, would at any time have shown that this is an alternative with which all communities have at one time or another been confronted.

Again, with regard to the case of Edward II, which constitutional historians used to cite as confirming the theory that parliament has a right to depose the king, Maitland points out that the actual facts do not support this view: " On the whole, as it seems to me, these proceedings, so far from strengthening the notion that a king might be legally deposed, demonstrated pretty clearly that there was nobody empowered by law to set the king aside."[1]

Similarly, with regard to the animating spirit of Courts of Justice and of Parliaments in the earlier days. The educational historian with his professional distrust of kings would have us believe that the only check upon their wickedness arose from the determination of the barons and tenants in chief to assemble together and

[1] Maitland's *Constitutional History*, pp. 60, 61 and 190.

HISTORY AS A SCIENCE

impose the necessary restrictions upon the dangerous growth of arbitrary powers, and that patriotic Englishmen in general regarded representation as a privilege to be coveted because it enabled them to secure justice for their fellow-countrymen. The facts are quite different. " We ought to remember that attendance at Court is no coveted privilege. We must be careful not to introduce the notions of modern times in which a seat in Parliament is eagerly desired. This would render a good deal of history unintelligible. . . . What seems to us from a modern point of view a valuable political right seemed to those who had it an onerous political obligation. The great baron again had no particular desire to be about his lord's court : if, as was too often the case, he was not very faithful to his lord, his lord's court was the very last place he would wish to be."[1] Both Maitland and Dicey agree that it was under the strong kings that courts and parliaments were made to perform useful work which they would otherwise have gladly shirked. Thus, when we get to the facts, we find that it was frequently the strong king (or tyrant) who keeps his eye upon his wickedly-inclined subjects rather than the subjects upon a wickedly-inclined king.

Such cases suggest that the advent of more accurate methods of observation will involve a readjustment of political values. The fear of despotism which impels the constitutional historian to " create precedent " of a contrary character, has caused in the public mind a miscalculation of the relative importance of the part played by the executive on the one hand and by parliament on the other. Mankind has no doubt suffered severely in the past from the misdeeds and extravagant pretensions of its rulers. It is intelligible, therefore, that the predominant desire of those interested in the story of humanity should be to discover an effectual means for preventing continued injustice of government. Con-

[1] Maitland's *Constitutional History*, page 62.

GOVERNMENT AND THE STUDY OF HISTORY 53

sequently historians have allowed themselves to be convinced that political evolution consists in little else than in the curtailment of royal authority and in the transference of power from king to parliament. They have accordingly come to believe that their attention should be mainly fixed upon the doings of political assemblies, since it is by their assistance that government has been induced to approximate to the supposed ideal type. That there are other features of government perhaps even more essential for national prosperity than its conversion to democratic uses does not seem to be thought of. The importance of senates and political assemblies, in fact, seems to be measured entirely by the gratitude which mankind in general, and particularly the English people, feel, because on certain occasions they have been instrumental in preserving them from the exercise of arbitrary power.

Gratitude, however, though an honourable motive, is a disturbing factor from the strictly scientific point of view, and may lead to a misapprehension of the forces engaged in the real work of government. In the present instance it has undoubtedly led historians to bestow exaggerated attention upon an institution which, evolutionally speaking, has played only a secondary part in political development, which is a subsequent accessory and not an original feature of government. By the flattery which has been bestowed upon them parliaments have been induced to believe that they are practically omnipotent ; and the disrepute into which parliamentary government is beginning to fall throughout the world is largely due to the exposure of unjustifiable pretensions. As a controlling power parliament is essential. But the power of control, however efficient, is unable to guarantee certain other most important features of good government which parliament does not supply but which, nevertheless, are accredited to it. It is half a century, for instance, since Sir John Seeley, among other corrections

54 HISTORY AS A SCIENCE

of popular fallacies on the subject of government, showed conclusively that legislation was not the work of Parliament but of the Cabinet. Yet his demonstration has been without effect, parliament is still habitually referred to as our great " legislative assembly," and one learned professor has publicly made lamentation because it is losing a legislative power which as a matter of fact it never possessed.

The determining considerations in this case are clear. It would be sadly inconsistent with the ultra-democratic principles which are so much the fashion if it were admitted that the important function of making laws belong to any other body than the representatives of the people. Especially is this so when the alternative is to attribute legislation to " distinguished individuals " who are out of favour at the present epoch, and to give the representatives of the nation no other part to play than that of saying " Aye " and " No ", which is all that Seeley leaves them. Nor can it be said that such an error is of little importance because it does not interfere with the effective work of a constitution. That is exactly the effect that it does tend to produce. A body which continually hears itself spoken of as a legislative assembly is tempted to try to justify its reputation and brings government into disrepute by its misplaced activity. In America especially both the Senate and the House of Representatives have shown themselves determined to prove that they are not called legislative assemblies for nothing, with the result that the transaction of really important business is impeded and both Houses of Congress at the end of a session are encumbered with piles of useless legislation. The injury thus caused to public interests has, according to some American authorities, attained the proportion of a great " scandal and oppression."

In conclusion, then, it must be held that an investigation into the functions of government on the strictest inductive principles is one of the most imperative needs

GOVERNMENT AND THE STUDY OF HISTORY 55

of the time, for two reasons. Unless the phenomena of government are studied without reference to any influence which the discovery of the actual facts may have upon political or other conduct, a proper science of history is impossible. In the second place, so long as our knowledge of the real functions of government remains as imperfect as it is at present, the charlatan has an open field for his wild and dangerous speculations, and even the honest and cautious reformer will be working in the dark. The evolution of government has taken place in close relation with the nature of man as he is and not as he ought to be, and its improvement cannot be effectively undertaken until we have gained an accurate conception of past history.

CHAPTER IV

WAR AND THE INDUCTIVE STUDY OF HISTORY

THE difficulty which attends the foundation of a science of history is more than ever apparent when we come to the subject of war. In common with other human phenomena it may be approached either from the point of view of science or from the point of view of morality. It may be regarded either as a phase of social evolution to be studied or as a moral aberration to be cured. Most historians never quite make up their minds which attitude to adopt, and the result is that a phenomenon which is of the very first importance from the sociological point of view does not receive the scientific attention which it deserves. Indeed, with social philosophers like Frederic Harrison and Lord Morley it arouses indignation as a crime against humanity rather than interest as a hitherto habitual feature of the intercourse of societies.

One of the best methods of curing a bad habit in an individual is to inspire him with the belief that he has it in his power to effect his own reform. Many writers upon morals and politics seem to think that the bad habit of making war may be cured in the same way. In their opinion war may be reckoned among those simple voluntary acts from which it is possible to abstain at will. Such a belief is unscientific as well as unpractical. It is unscientific because it is based upon the wholly incorrect assumption that the psychology of the nation is identical with the psychology of the individual, and will respond to similar treatment. It is

56

WAR AND THE STUDY OF HISTORY 57

unscientific, because the unbroken record of hostilities in the past is deliberately overlooked in accordance with the educational method in the hope of strengthening the moral appeal. It is unpractical, because the cure of undesirable national habits depends not upon impassioned argument, but upon measures taken after careful and scientific study of the symptoms.

A scientific study of history depends among other things upon a comprehension of the nature of the social organism. War is one of the most incessant and important activities in which the social organism engages ; and to treat war merely as a moral delinquency is to shut ourselves off from a valuable source of information as to that nature. It is to prohibit a line of inquiry indispensable for an understanding of the causes and conditions of human progress. So important, indeed, is the influence which the struggle of societies has exercised upon history that it must be regarded as an indispensable feature of any inquiry into the method by which social evolution has taken place. To begin the study of history without giving its proper place to this phenomenon is like attempting to explain the movements of the heavenly bodies without considering the laws of gravitation, or the elements of chemistry without regard to the laws of molecular attraction and repulsion. With the progressive portion of mankind the tendency to war has been in historical times universal and invariable. Throughout the whole of the recorded history of mankind, there has never been any considerable nation that has not been incessantly involved in war. On inductive principles the conclusion is obvious. The tendency to indulge in war must be regarded as one of the characteristics with which a society is naturally and originally endowed : it is an impulse which is instinctive and which has a strong natural sanction behind it. So clear is the evidence, scientifically speaking, upon this point, that nothing less than some pecu-

58 HISTORY AS A SCIENCE

liar obsession of the human mind could have prevented
the admission of the truth. This obsession, as the reader
knows, is the educational theory of life and history. To
admit that war is a phenomenon possessing a serious
scientific interest would increase, so it is thought, the
tendency to its indulgence by giving an evolutional
sanction to a morally reprehensible practice.

In the foundation of a science it is necessary at the
outset to distinguish between the more relevant and the
less relevant facts, to discover which are the most important or the mainly determining principles of many
presented to our view. Astronomy, physics, chemistry,
have all owed their development to the discovery of
some such principle by means of a hypothesis which
was found to account for the disposition which the
phenomena assumed. As already pointed out in a previous chapter, the only way in which to introduce order
into the apparently unrelated and incoherent details of
the combined lives of nations and individuals is to
follow the same procedure, to assume for the time being
the superior importance of one or two given phenomena,
and then to study the facts afresh in order to see whether
this judgment is confirmed or no. From the point of
view of inductive science the inveteracy of the habit
of war marks it out as a phenomenon of this character.
The antagonism of societies has absorbed such an enormous part of the activities of the human race from
the beginning of history up to the present day that no
unbiased observer can have the slightest doubt that it
constitutes one of those determining principles to which
reference has been made.

But the obstacles which the educational instinct places
in the way of the scientific study of international relations are very formidable. The jurist assists the moralist
and the historian in obscuring the real issues. From the
point of view of the jurist, war is merely an unfortunate
consequence of a disputed question of right or wrong.

WAR AND THE STUDY OF HISTORY 59

In consequence of a false analogy with individual life it is assumed that war arises merely from a difference of opinion, which leads to fighting because there is no other means of settling the dispute. It is therefore something that can easily be avoided by eliminating causes of dispute by reducing armaments, or by popularizing some form of arbitration. In the absence of any common authority which can adjudicate in the matter, as the international lawyers say, nations are compelled to have recourse to the organized power of the community to enforce their view of what is right.

To the evolutionist this is a solution which savours more of the refinements of civilization than of the truth of nature, a sophisticated interpretation of the phenomenon devised to meet the legal and moral requirements of an educated humanity. To him it seems evident that war is the result of a practically irresistible tendency inherent in the structure of societies which urges them to a trial of strength quite independently of the existence of any disputed question of right and wrong. Nations in this respect and in many others are primitive organisms, and like primitive organisms they fight with or without reason. Those who are in the habit of carrying their observation beneath the conventionally moral aspect of things will find abundant evidence all tending to show that in the vast majority of cases it is not the dispute which engenders the warlike feeling, but the previous existence of a warlike feeling which engenders the dispute. The fact that some question of justice is almost invariably alleged as the cause of difference is no proof that such a question actually exists, but merely shows that we have arrived at a stage of civilization where decency demands that the real motive should be covered by a moral pretext. The evolutionist whose business it is to trace the primitive instinct beneath the moral or legal refinements by which it has been overlaid, is compelled to regard the ques-

60 HISTORY AS A SCIENCE

tion of relative superiority as the prevalent cause of the conflict of nations. The existence and pretensions of one nation are incompatible with the existence and pretensions of another, and a decision is sought by war. War is a struggle for supremacy and the idea of justice is a subsequently imported consideration which, evolutionally speaking, has no place among the original motives which have urged nations against one another. Under the original dispensation of nature there is no question of justice, but merely of survival, and it is by this rule that we must in the first instance seek to interpret the relation of communities to one another.

It has been a permanent feature of the international situation in the past that no active nation has ever been content with its position and prospects, however good they might be. There has always been something wrong either in imagination or reality. Since 1870 the position of Germany seemed to the general European public eminently satisfactory. Not so, however, to its rulers and people. The Germans made war because they were dissatisfied with their place in the sun, or rather because, according to the Emperor and his advisers, they had no place in the sun at all. And so it has been throughout the history of the world. Every nation has sought to increase its strength and extend its dominions at the cost of every other nation, and it is essential not merely to the foundation of a proper science of history but to the practical reformation of the world that this truth should be recognized. It was the mistake of President Wilson that he persisted in adopting the educational standpoint in his view of the case. In one of the documents, presumably written or inspired by him, in which he endeavoured to shape the European situation conformably to his high ideals at the time of the Peace Conference, reference was made " to the now discarded theory that nations are engaged in a struggle for supremacy." This is the method already discussed

WAR AND THE STUDY OF HISTORY 61

of attempting to bring about a change of character by assuming that it has already taken place. President Wilson, in fact, hoped to educate the world into the adoption of a higher standard of international action, and it was essential to the success of such an effort that no natural sanction should be alleged for what had hitherto been the customary attitude.

In support of this contention that to make war or to abstain from war is not the simple matter of resolute determination that moralists and educational historians would have us believe, it is useful to remember that scientific observation reveals the existence of certain psychological peculiarities which are the outcome, not of the will of the individuals taken separately, but of those individuals acting as a mass. Under certain circumstances individual feeling is quite powerless to make headway against mass feeling. A nation, in fact, has certain characteristics and tendencies not consisting of the sum of the characteristics of the individuals who compose it, but having a sort of corporate origin ; and over these tendencies the individual as an individual has no control. Forty years ago, in a work devoted to national psychology and the study of crowds, the present writer attempted to explain the low standard of international morality on the theory that the morality of crowds applied under certain conditions to all large bodies of men, including nations. It was suggested that we have here an explanation of the startling paradox that beings, amenable to reason and decency in their private relations, should, under the influence of national emotion, that is to say mass emotion, act like beings in the lowest stages of barbarity. Though the reception subsequently accorded to the work of the French writer, M. le Bon, showed that the theory of the crowd was generally accepted, neither he nor anyone else—so far as the present writer is aware—has ever developed the idea that a study of crowd morality may be capable

HISTORY AS A SCIENCE

of throwing valuable light upon international affairs and the method of dealing with them.

The reason for this has already been stated. The idea of undertaking such a study is unpopular because it tends to weaken the philanthropical belief in the power of any nation to abstain from war. It would be to insinuate that men are not under all circumstances lords of themselves and masters of their fate. The notion of regarding the individual merely as a part of a larger organism, to whose will his own is occasionally subordinate, and at whose behest he must occasionally move, is an idea which the educational historian and the moral reformer will not entertain. War is the result of the machinations of kings and capitalists and designing statesmen, and to study it as a matter of national as distinct from individual psychology is to tamper with moral principle.

Yet it is along this line of inquiry that there is the best hope of gaining knowledge which will enable us to deal successfully with the subject in the future. Psychologically speaking, it is not the individual who is responsible for war but the nation : war is the result of a social, not an individual, emotion. The machinations of kings or statesmen may have added one or two to the interminable list of international conflicts ; but the impetus thus given to the militarism of nations is an entirely negligible influence in comparison with that which arises from the mere proximity of two active and ambitious societies. If we wish to attain practical results we must abandon the educational method with its feeble pretence that accommodation has always been possible in national quarrels, and frankly recognize the verdict of inductive observation, that ordeal by battle has been the inevitable outcome of the rivalry of social organisms. It is impossible to count, as the philanthropists do, upon the individual horror of war as a means of ending war : the feelings of a given number

WAR AND THE STUDY OF HISTORY 63

of people taken separately are no indication of what their feelings may be when acting as a nation. A mass decision is generally much lower, morally speaking, than the decision which each of the individuals composing the mass would have given if they had been able to deliver it in actual or mental isolation. And from this two results follow. In the first place, a mass or crowd cannot be deterred from carrying out a certain course by the same arguments that would have deterred the individual from so doing. As the decision or impulse is a mass decision or impulse, it can only be arrested by the application of motives or deterrents or inducements which appeal to the mass. Psychologically the point is this, that the law—whatever it may be—which determines the action of the mass or crowd dominates for the time being the law which guides the action of the individual. The ordinary mentality of the individual becomes merged in the mentality of the mass or social organism. The appeal to the individual is of no avail because it is impossible to detach him from his surroundings, which, for the time being, as it were, destroy his individuality.

In the second place, since the morality of the mass is on a lower plane than that of the individuals who compose it, it will frequently form resolutions and carry out a line of conduct from which its individual components would shrink as individuals. A nation must be regarded as a mass from this point of view, and in this peculiarity we find the explanation of the fact that in the conduct of foreign policy things are habitually done and applauded which men would not dream of doing in private life. Here, too, we may find the reason why war, though condemned by the vast majority of the individuals of the world, almost we might say by the whole of these individuals, still incessantly goes on. Though the majority of individuals in every civilized nation may on a given occasion dislike and detest the idea of war,

HISTORY AS A SCIENCE

their detestation is not sufficiently strong to prevail against the tendency of the mass or nation to make war.

As the present writer has elsewhere shown,[1] civilized human beings live two lives, one as individuals and one as members of a political body, their interests as individuals being frequently quite different from their interests as members of a nation. As individuals they may condemn war, but as members of a nation they feel compelled to wage it. The national point of view at the time of an international crisis dominates the individual point of view, or rather it causes the individual point of view to cease to exist. Accordingly, a nation may not merely go to war though a large number of its members dislike the idea of war : we have the further paradox that it may go to war though the majority of its members dislike the idea of war : it may even go to war though the whole of its members, if questioned as individuals, would say that they objected to war : and it would go to war because this theoretical individual point of view had ceased to exist, being superseded by the mass or national view which has the greater weight of instinctive hereditary force behind it. Under these circumstances a motive which is to stop war must be something coarser and more practical, even more brutal, than would have been necessary in the individual case.

It is not necessary to dispute the value of high international ideas for the moral education of mankind. But to effect any real change in national habits some more cogent influence must be brought into play. The weakness of the League of Nations consists in this, that it sets its appeal too high, and uses arguments the very nobility of which renders them incapable of affecting national sentiment. It is frequently assumed that the exhibition by some great nation of a palpable reluctance to go to war will induce other nations to follow suit.

[1] *Conditions of National Success.*

WAR AND THE STUDY OF HISTORY 65

Unfortunately experience shows that a conspicuous disinclination to put the matter to the test of force tends to produce exactly the opposite effect. A nation, even so unimportant a nation as that of the Turks, provided it is prepared to fight when other nations are not, is completely master of the situation. It was a knowledge of this unpleasant truth which enabled the Turks to defy victorious Europe after the Great War; and which caused Mussolini, in the matter of his attack upon the Greeks, to ignore the authority of the League of Nations to which he nominally belonged. In short, if any practical result is to be effected, it is becoming more and more clear that we must rely chiefly upon self-interest in the work of international reform, since self-interest is, and must long remain, the determining motive of national action.

Such an idea will be regarded as uninspiring when compared with the brilliant hopes that have recently been held out. Yet it would seem to be at least more scientific than a scheme of reform which counts upon the sudden cessation of an unbroken record of national self-seeking. No radical change can yet be expected in national psychology. Crude as the idea may seem, the only method of bringing war to an end, or rather of making a commencement of bringing war to an end, is for those nations who are contented with their present position and prospects to have an arrangement or virtual understanding with one another for the purpose of preventing a recourse to arms by those who hope to profit by fresh international disturbance. Only in this way can we gain that interval of peace during which the world may become accustomed to those higher international ideals which cannot hope to find immediate acceptance. There must be a combination, not merely of nations who profess an academic interest in the maintenance of peace as do the members of the League, but of those nations who for definite and specific reasons

HISTORY AS A SCIENCE

are interested in avoiding war. An arrangement with this end in view does not call for an aggressively armed coalition, but merely for an understanding between those who have most to lose by a renewal of hostilities. The nations to which these conditions most obviously apply are those who were recent allies, and more particularly England, France, Belgium, Poland, and America.

It will probably be objected that such an understanding implies a coalition against one of the most intellectual nations of this or of any time, Germany. Unfortunately the Germans have other qualities besides intellect. Their conduct of the war, and indeed their history since 1870, shows that they have a double measure of that brutal self-assertion which we are justified in saying is out of place among the nations of the twentieth century. According to the present theory, the desire of nations to extend their power is an original evolutional instinct which has been useful in the past. It is equally certain, however, that a period arrives when the further progress of civilization depends upon its disappearance. To many people that period seemed to have arrived as early as the middle of the nineteenth century. England had her peace exhibition, and it is well known that the desire of the French people to inaugurate a new era by relaxing the military preparations was one of the chief causes that led to her defeat in 1870. The Germans alone, instead of conforming to the changed requirements of a progressive civilization, openly professed before the whole of Europe an adherence to the gospel of blood and iron, and when the opportunity seemed to have arrived, carried their principles into practice. If, therefore, in any future attempts to secure international harmony the chief nations of the world seem to be discriminating against them, they have only themselves to blame.

Again, it may be urged that such a coalition implies an unjustifiable assumption of superior merit on the

WAR AND THE STUDY OF HISTORY 67

part of those who would form it. The Allies, it will be said, in acting thus, would assume the position of the elect, and would proceed to lay down laws for the rest of the world merely because they happened to be victors in the recent war. The answer to such reasoning is that the situation which confronts the world is so threatening that we cannot stop to consider refinements such as this. It is impossible to take efficient steps for putting things right without hurting somebody's feelings, and those who brought about the world conflagration hardly have the right to complain if they are the people whose feelings are hurt, especially if by encouraging a braggart like Hitler they make it clear to all the world that they will start another war as soon as they see the remotest chance of gaining anything from it. When the Germans begin to carry out the promises of amendment which have been made for them—they have made none for themselves—it will be time enough to consider the question of restoratives for their wounded self-esteem. We cannot afford to look coldly upon a scheme which promises peace merely because it falls short of the requirements of ideal justice. Throughout the history of political evolution self-interest has been a more powerful agent of progress than altruism, and a beginning of improvement in international conditions will be effected by the same motive or not at all.

Doubtless it will be pointed out that according to the principles upon which the present argument is based, all nations are in a last analysis equally responsible for the prevalence of war, because it is the result of an all-pervading evolutional impulse ; to discriminate, therefore, against certain particular nations on account of a practice of which all are guilty is, in the highest degree, unjust. The answer in this case also is the same as before, that we are dealing with a question of practical politics, and must frame our measures accordingly. The object is not to fix responsibility for the misfortunes of

68   HISTORY AS A SCIENCE

the past, but to prevent their repetition. Though all nations have indulged in war, some have now arrived at a stage where they are ready to abandon the practice, and it is obviously in the interests of civilization that these should have every possible encouragement. Others again, like Russia, Germany and Turkey, are frankly determined to revive the old state of things if they think they have anything to gain by it. Nothing will alter this difference of national outlook, and any practical scheme of reform must take it into account. The difficulty with the League of Nations is that while it contains communities who are really and earnestly in favour of peace, it also contains others who are not, but who join merely in the hope of being able to make something out of the venture, or because they would incur embarrassing suspicion if they remained outside. In other words, there is nothing to prevent any League of Nations having within it some dishonest members who are there, not for the purpose of ensuring peace, but because outward conformity has its advantages; members who, like Italy, are ready, if it suits them, to commit unjustifiable acts of war in defiance of their solemn pledges, and who threaten instant resignation if the slightest intention is manifested of calling them to account. Clearly the best way of remedying this defect is to reinforce the League of Nations by the creation of some additional body whose members, from the circumstances of the case, not only find their greatest advantage in a state of peace but are prepared to go to considerable trouble in order to secure it. If we are ever to make a start in the task of bringing war to an end, such an organization is the only one which can be trusted not to fall to pieces the moment the real test comes.

Not so long ago there were many who accused not Germany but France of being, through the alliances she has formed, the cause of the present unrest, and who

WAR AND THE STUDY OF HISTORY 69

went so far as to assert that her conduct showed her to be aiming at the hegemony of Europe from which Germany has just been displaced. The most obvious answer to such an indictment is that France, with her dwindling population, has not got the slightest chance of establishing a military supremacy, and knows it. Any French statesman who cherished such an ambition in the face of the feeble numbers and failing birth-rate of France would be immediately recognized by his country-men as insane. The real truth, of course, is that the policy of the French, which seems to be inspired by ambition, is in reality dictated by justifiable fears. The French, after incurring desperate losses in a war from which others have reaped the greater advantage, were left without protection in the immediate proximity of a strong, vindictive and relentless enemy. They there-fore determined to take on their own account such measures as seemed necessary for safety in the absence of an international guarantee. Objections, however, against an international guarantee have been raised on the ground that the world has undergone a miraculous conversion since the War, that Germany has for ever relinquished the fondly cherished dreams which came so near realization, and that a renewal of the system of alliances would revive the military feeling of Europe which is on the point of disappearing.

The great advantage of the American view that France is in no need of military alliances and precautions is that it saves so much trouble and relieves those who hold it from any unpleasant obligations in the matter. Assume that there has been, or that there presently will be, a sudden change in the psychology of nations, assume that the historic disposition of Germany has been completely altered since 1918, and we at once get rid of the notion that France is in need of any especial support. A theory which while breathing the loftiest humanity, ensures the avoidance of any self-denying exertion, has undeniable

70 HISTORY AS A SCIENCE

attractions. Nations, like individuals, are never so convinced of the propriety of a certain course as when it coincides with their selfish inclinations. Fortunately for the future of Europe, and of mankind, the British government decided to wait no longer for the assistance which the world had every right to expect from America, but have independently promised to come to the aid of France if attacked.

It is not, in fact, generally perceived that the necessity of placing France beyond the fear of attack is a vital interest of all nations who desire peace. The quarrel between France and Germany is not a mere private feud as the pacifists pretend, affecting these two rival nations alone, but a public matter which concerns the whole world, and for the following reasons. Though the immediate objective of Germany in the Great War was France, her real aim was first the conquest of the British Empire, and then, absurd as it may now seem, of the world. They, themselves, have repeatedly admitted it. An unrestricted course of self-adulation had convinced the Germans that when once they had achieved the comparatively easy conquest of the insufficiently defended British Empire a world supremacy would be theirs. But though England was the goal of their endeavour, France stood in the way ; it was necessary to pass through France on their way to England. France, in short, was attacked for the purpose of facilitating the conquest of more dangerous and hated rivals, who had blundered into the possession of an Empire which they were too weak to hold. It was a manifest decree of Providence that imperial opportunities such as the British possessed should belong only to the cleverest, bravest, hardiest and noblest of living nations, which was in this case, of course, the Germans themselves. The attack on France in 1914 was merely the opening phase of an attempt to conquer the British Empire and win a world supremacy. Only by ignoring this aspect of the matter is it pos-

WAR AND THE STUDY OF HISTORY 71

sible for anyone to pretend that the relations of France with Germany are the concern of France alone.

English Liberals have always loudly proclaimed the pacific disposition of their party, and in particular are convinced that it is owing to their superior sense and virtue that the nation has been kept free from what they pretend to regard as the degradation of universal military service. Yet every student of military history is aware that the immunity which Liberals claim to have secured for their country is in reality due to geographical circumstances. It is the interposition of France between Germany and her real object which since 1870 has been the decisive influence in relieving England from the arduous military and financial burdens that would otherwise have been entailed. But for the existence of France we should for the last fifty years have been face to face with an envious and powerful rival, whose immediate proximity would have altered the whole outlook of English political life, and would undoubtedly have forced us to become that pitiable thing, a conscript nation ; a rival who would doubtless have found time and means to develop carefully and scientifically the fleet which even in its imperfect state was so dangerously efficient in the late war ; a rival who would have compelled even the Labour Party to contemplate the necessity of military preparations adequate for the protection of the nation and the empire.

To an impartial international critic, reviewing the whole circumstances, the truth would be clear that the task of watching the common enemy and of making adequate preparations for the inevitable struggle was left almost entirely to France. When the storm actually broke, slowly and much against the wishes of radical politicians, and in the face of " an invincible refusal on the part of the majority of the Cabinet to contemplate British intervention by force of arms,"[1] we came to

[1] Winston Churchill's *World Crisis.*

F

HISTORY AS A SCIENCE

the assistance of France with an army the numerical inadequacy of which was not compensated by its very great efficiency. Our subsequent exertions, indeed, were of a kind unequalled in the history of the world. But that does not alter the fact that the initial shock was far greater than the French should have been called upon to bear alone, nor the further fact that the task of continually " guarding the pass," of continually living under the military dispensation and more exacting type of government necessary for those who are liable at any moment to be invaded was for decades the portion of France, while England was entirely free from the perpetual strain entailed by these indispensable defensive arrangements.

But the full account of our responsibility for the plight of our neighbours is not exhausted even now. Though the accident which has given the French a frontier open to the common foe would have made their position perilous enough in any case, it has now to be pointed out that the traditional policy of Great Britain has in another way rendered that position more perilous still. France, according to the commonly received opinion, is supposed to have drawn the unoffending people of England into a desperate continental quarrel which they magnanimously made their own. That we had any share in precipitating the attack upon France is an idea which the majority of thinkers would summarily dismiss as absurd. Yet in the judgment of posterity we will not be held altogether guiltless. It is one of the favourite boasts of our publicists and politicians that the British Empire is not a military empire, but that on the contrary military expenditure and preparation has always been reduced to the barest minimum. Those who make this proud claim do our democracy and its rulers somewhat less than justice. The truth is that the military preparation necessary for the defence of the empire has been habitually reduced not merely to

WAR AND THE STUDY OF HISTORY 73

the barest minimum but below it. To the average observer it might seem that if a nation chooses to take undue risks that is its own affair. But neither in the individual nor international world is liability so limited. A man is considered guilty of an offence against the community if he encourages burglars by the habitual display of insufficiently guarded wealth, and the same principle applies to international matters. Especially is this the case where a nation is in possession of a priceless imperial property which another nation, known to be unscrupulous as well as strong, openly covets. The relations between Germany and the British Empire were of this kind; and the temptation carelessly offered by the sight of an inadequately defended empire eventually proved irresistible. So true is this that the outbreak of the Great War may in a large measure be attributed to the conviction of the German people that the richest prize in the world was practically within their grasp, since it was in the hands of a nation in their opinion too self-indulgent to take the measures necessary for its defence. History shows that nothing fosters international unrest so much as great possessions weakly held, and the French may very well make the point against us that the inadequacy of our defensive imperial organization had a disastrous, even a decisive, share in arousing the cupidity of the Germans, and inflaming their determination to commence the world war by their onslaught upon France.

All the preceding arguments except the last apply to America; with a somewhat diminished force it is true, but they apply nevertheless. America, in fact, is under an obligation to two countries, while we are only under an obligation to one. Just as France defended the interests of England, so have England and France defended the interests of Americans, and have relieved the United States from the necessity at one time or another of fighting for the retention of their present

HISTORY AS A SCIENCE

position and privileges. But for the desperate resistance of the Allies, the " Admiral of the Atlantic " might even now be on his way to found a South American empire, the Monroe Doctrine might be relegated to the domain of impertinent futilities, and a dangerous enemy established in the neighbourhood of the Great Republic. In preventing the possibility of any such occurrence, in maintaining a defensive struggle in which all in the last analysis are equally concerned, in the work of defending the world, for that is what it amounts to, France has been permanently maimed, the British Empire seriously, though temporarily, disabled, and the United States hardly hurt at all.

Like the English, however, Americans are led by that ignorance of the psychological causes of war which the educational theory fosters, to assume that the quarrels of Europe are quarrels which concern Europe alone, while the apprehension of actual danger, which might have quickened their perceptions, is prevented by their distance from the scene of trouble. The idea, therefore, of owing gratitude to France and England for what they have done is more absurd to the majority of Americans than the idea of owing gratitude to France is to many Englishmen. Of their own chivalrous free will they came to the assistance of the Allies in their sore distress, and they look for the recognition which is due to the voluntary saviours of the world. To themselves they seem to have done all, and more than all, that could be expected of them, and so long as this state of mind lasts, Europe and the League of Nations may look in vain for the assistance that they have every right to expect.

As we might have anticipated, a lofty moral excuse is alleged by the Americans for pursuing a course of inaction which they had determined upon for quite other reasons. They have, indeed, been even more successful than the British in popularizing a view of their case which depicts them in the noblest light. The argument

WAR AND THE STUDY OF HISTORY 75

upon which they chiefly rely is that their history shows them to be of a higher moral calibre than the rest of the world because they have never indulged any military ambitions, and for this reason they are absolved from any obligation to help Europe in escaping from the troubles which it has brought upon itself.

To the dispassionate observer it seems absurd for any nation to put forward such pretensions when it has, as a matter of fact, fought several desperate wars ; the Americans declare, however, that in every case where they have engaged in hostilities they were compelled by the dictates of self-respect to act as they did ; and they seek to confirm this belief in their superior morality by pointing to the fact that one state in the American Union does not make war upon another. At this rate we shall presently have the French claiming credit because the Department of the Seine does not attack the Department of the Loire, or the English demanding the admiration of the world because Yorkshire does not invade Lancashire to avenge a defeat at cricket. Such sophistry is only rendered possible by the ambiguity of the word State. The term State is an identical name which may be given to two perfectly different kinds of political entities, having one meaning in Europe and another in America. In Europe it used to designate a separate political organism animated with the real though latent hostility which diverse social organisms always feel towards one another. In America it means merely a department of a homogeneous political body. The fact that the " states " of America are not only radically akin but have for 150 years owed allegiance to the same political authority, which is the really vital feature of the situation, is left entirely out of sight.

Even if such an argument were not palpably fallacious, the assertion that the American States have never made war upon one another is untrue. For it so happens that within the memory of some still living they have

76 HISTORY AS A SCIENCE

fought the most desperate civil war in history. If the Americans really possessed the superiority of character to which in this matter they lay claim, here surely in a civil dispute between two portions of a united body politic they would have found the opportunity to set a noble example to the world by showing that even vital differences may be satisfactorily composed without having recourse to " methods of barbarism." But no ; with a determination strangely resembling that of other nations in a similar position, the Americans decided that there was nothing for it but to engage in a war of which the horror, from the point of view which we are now considering, was increased by the fact that it was fratricidal, and that it caused losses which have seriously, perhaps fatally, impoverished their best racial strain.

They remain, however, quite undismayed by all attempts to convict them of inconsistency. In fact, their attitude to their own civil war against England, which they call the War of Independence, affords a typical instance of the way in which they are in the habit not merely of begging disputed questions in their own favour, but of entirely reversing their point of view when they find it convenient to do so. If we disregard certain unessential features of the struggle between North and South, both of these wars were fought for the preservation of a great, important and beneficial political union. The English fought as they had every right to do in order that their countrymen in America should remain within the British political union. The Americans of the North fought as they had every right to do, in order that their countrymen in the South should remain within the American political union. Yet while the Americans claim that their action on this occasion was inspired by a great and noble purpose, while Abraham Lincoln and General Grant are made the subject of inordinate adulation, the English generals and statesmen who sought to hold the colonists to their allegiance are

WAR AND THE STUDY OF HISTORY   77

condemned as the instruments of an unjust and wicked tyranny. The desire to maintain a political union is noble when upheld by Americans, but infamous when upheld by the English. If the desire for a separate jurisdiction was dishonourable in the one case, it was equally dishonourable in the other. The fact that the sea intervened between the two portions of the British political community, while in America the dissentient parts were contiguous, has no bearing whatever upon the moral, legal or political aspect of the case, whatever effect it may have had upon the practical result. It is idle to attempt to escape from the charge of warguiltiness on the plea that when you make war upon a certain issue it is right, when others make war upon the same issue it is wrong.

But though it cannot be admitted that the Americans are in any way free from the operation of the psychological causes which engender war, or have shown any hesitation in promoting where necessary their national interests by warlike means, they can certainly plead that no other nation possessing such enormous power has ever been so moderate in its exercise. Geographical reasons entirely account for this. Most nations would be able to lay claim to a similar moderation if they could get all they want without fighting. The impartial historian is compelled to take notice of the circumstance that everything which a nation could desire has been automatically given to the Americans by the bounty of nature and their fortunate international situation; and that they have only been moderate in the exercise of strength where there has been no reason to act otherwise. The main cause of aggressive war is the desire for expansion, which is a corollary of the desire for supremacy, and it is worthy of remark that the Americans have behaved precisely like other nations when they have met with obstacles to what may justly be called their imperial aims. As Lord Charnwood has

78 HISTORY AS A SCIENCE

pointed out in this connection, " the process of expansion included at one time acts more discreditable than any of at all comparable magnitude which can be charged to the British Empire." And again : " Americans who censure the imperialism of other nations might do well to recall many chapters in the history of their own." Their slate is very far from being clean with regard to Texas, California, New Mexico, and Arizona. The amicable disposition of the Americans as a nation would, in fact, seem to last just so long as things are going as they wish, and no longer.

It might have been supposed, too, that in this twentieth century the real proof of a hatred of war would be a conspicuous readiness to join the League of Nations. To put a seal to their ceaseless professions of pacifism by entering the great temple of peace would seem to be the most natural course under the circumstances. Such, however, is not the view taken by the majority of Americans who give many reasons for their abstention except the true one. Membership of an international society where all are equal is not compatible with their firmly held conviction that in spite of their unenviable record in murder, drunkenness and divorce they are morally the leaders of the world. To submit to the jurisdiction of the League would be to admit that they had no greater claim to consideration than England. That would be bad enough ; but as the case stands it would be even worse. Since every self-governing nation has a vote, it follows that each of the leading colonies of the British Empire is entitled to rank as a separate nation, and to have a vote equal to that of America. From the War of Independence to the presidency of Woodrow Wilson, jealousy of England, to put it very mildly, has been the dominant motive of American foreign policy. The idea, therefore, of being outvoted by that very conglomeration of nations over whom they claim to have established so decisive a lead

WAR AND THE STUDY OF HISTORY 79

in everything which appertains to a higher civilization cannot for a moment be entertained. However paltry such a sentiment may be, its existence has got to be recognized. Nothing will ever induce America to join the League so long as this state of things continues, and therefore no substantial progress can be made with schemes of world peace until it is altered. Voting power according to white population is the most feasible idea. It would be a truly charitable act if British statesmanship could arrange the vote of the Empire on these terms, and so help Americans to escape from a position which is bringing upon them the unsparing condemnation of Europe and of posterity.

According to the present view, then, the position revealed by a scientific study of international relations is as follows. All nations in consequence of the psychological nature of social organisms are predisposed to war. The Americans are the only nation in history who have ever pretended to be exempt from this tendency, and their claim will not bear a moment's impartial examination. It follows from this that nations, by their own unaided efforts, are unable to abstain from war, and that the schemes of those who hope by voluntary means to bring the practice of war to an end will be inoperative unless supplemented by other measures adapted to the nature of the case. The League of Nations is an institution of the greatest value for enabling the world to become accustomed to the possibility of accommodating national rivalries and disputes without recourse to war. That, however, is the limit of its usefulness at present, because it is entirely without power to enforce its decisions. The only arrangement which has had the slightest really stabilizing influence on the international situation since the War has been the promise of the British Government to come to the aid of France in case of necessity. Exhortation and reasoning such as take place at the League meetings are not altogether useless, but

HISTORY AS A SCIENCE

they will not have the slightest real efficacy unless conditions can be secured in which they will have a chance of being carried into practice.

At the present crisis of the world's history the indispensable thing is to ensure an abstention from war of sufficient duration to enable the rising generation to appreciate the teaching of reason upon this subject. This breathing space in which the world may have time, as it were, to think things over can only be secured by the formation of an alliance among those nations who have a real and definite interest in the maintenance of peace : those nations, in short, who have quite obviously nothing to gain by further warfare. Such a defensive league would not constitute an unjustifiable assumption of power, as the pacifists pretend, destined to produce new wars ; it would be the best method of preventing them, because the scheme is based upon a knowledge of the psychological principles which underlie the relations of communities to one another. The morality of nations is on a lower plane than that of individuals, and will therefore respond only to a lower stimulus.

Though the conditions described represent the relation between nations and individuals at the present day, it is not necessary to hold that the lower morality of the nation will always dominate the higher morality of the individual. Without weakening the present argument it may be allowed that social evolution is taking a course under which the present conditions will be reversed, and the higher morality of the individual will eventually dominate the lower morality of the nation. But that era is still a very long way off, and to act as if it had already arrived is a procedure which invites disaster. According to theories elsewhere expounded, the progress of the world has been due to the development of the nation ; except under the protection of national principles, a civilization favouring the individual

WAR AND THE STUDY OF HISTORY 81

could not have been built up. National ideas are woven into the very texture of humanity. To expect that men who are what they are in consequence of the influence of national ideas, who owe all their moral and intellectual finish to the shaping they have received under the impulse of patriotism and the discipline of national training, should suddenly in a moment of time, evolutionally speaking, throw off the whole psychological environment in which through ages they have been nurtured, and take to new ways and ideas, is unthinkable. Even though a hollow international truce might be secured for a time, sooner or later there would be a reversion to those impulses which have the sanction of perhaps ten thousand years behind them. The grip of national emotions is too strong to be dispelled by the mere preaching of pacifist doctrine. Unless behind the League of Nations there is some other scheme upon which it may count for assistance, failure is certain. A virtual alliance of those who are satisfied with the present apportionment of worldly blessings, and are ready to combine for its maintenance, is the most practical method of procuring that period of repose from national scheming which is the necessary preliminary to a new order of international relations.

CHAPTER V

REVOLUTION AND THE INDUCTIVE STUDY OF HISTORY

THE way in which a strictly scientific study of the phenomenon of revolution should be conducted can best be illustrated by discussing a well-known work, Mrs. Webster's *French Revolution*. For Mrs. Webster's deliberate abandonment of the educational attitude, adopted by all previous writers on this subject, is an excellent example of the inductive method in history. With a scrupulous exactitude she places the facts before us for re-examination, passes once more under review the character and motives of the leading spirits, investigates anew the origin of the chief disturbances, and asks us candidly whether " this carnival of political malice, these forged misunderstandings between government and people, this blood-stained orgy of mingled fanaticism and crime, can really be made to bear the interpretation commonly placed upon it."

Before dealing with the further aspects of the case, it will be useful to recapitulate, as shortly as possible, some instances of the way in which popular beliefs as to the nature and origin of certain of the most celebrated occurrences in this revolution have been upset, by the simple method of making those occurrences speak for themselves, as it were, rather than transmit an interpretation which has been forced upon them.

It is conclusively shown that whatever the sufferings of the French people were, they had " certainly not reached that pitch of exasperation which, according to

REVOLUTION AND THE STUDY OF HISTORY 83

certain historians, would account for the excesses of the French Revolution "[1] (p. 5), that substantial reforms had commenced thirteen years before the popular outbreak (p. 6). That in 1789 there was " no element of sedition or disaffection towards the monarchy (p. 8), that the famine of 1789 was not so much real as apprehended, and that in so far as it was real it was artificially created (pp. 16–19, 132) : that Reveillon was attacked because he was obnoxious to the conspirators (p. 44) : that during the first four weeks of the opening of the " States General " not a word was said on the subject of the famine or the sufferings of the people (p. 46) : that Mirabeau acted as an *agent provocateur* (pp. 55, 56, etc.) : that rioting was not the spontaneous thing it is generally supposed to have been, but was deliberately fostered by organized desperadoes (pp. 39, 67, 68, etc.) : that Danton was not an honest revolutionary (pp. 71, 72, etc.) : that the Bastille was no monument of despotism and that the assault upon it was carried on to the cries of " Vive le Roi " (pp. 80, 98) : that the only honest outbreak under an honest man in the history of the Revolution was due to a mistake (pp. 87, 88) : that Foullon and Berthier were worthy, even noble men (pp. 58, 73, 97) : that the people desired peace and order, but were led astray by " calumny, corruption and terror," and that the object of the agitators was to exterminate anyone who encouraged contentment with the old regime (pp. 111–16) : that, generally speaking, the revolutionary movement was directed not to secure reform but to prevent it (p. 120, etc.) : that the famous march on Versailles was not caused by the emotion of " thirty millions of people spurning at slavery and demanding liberty," but was an Orleanistic conspiracy (p. 118) : that the celebrated champion of liberty, Madame Roland, was bent on preventing any practical schemes of reform, and that her political enthusiasm was largely inspired by personal envy and class hatred (pp. 204–8,

[1] Mrs. Webster's *French Revolution*, first edition.

84 HISTORY AS A SCIENCE

237, etc.) ; that many of the nobility were model and philanthropic landowners (p. 290) : that Danton in his celebrated words, " Toujours de l'audace," gave the signal for the September massacres (p. 305).

It is unnecessary to multiply these references. One more incident, however, will now be specially mentioned, because it shows better, perhaps, than any other the perverse spirit of deliberate misunderstanding with which the French Revolution has generally been studied. The famous Marseillais, whose memory has hitherto been enshrined in the hearts of all lovers of humanity, were not a band of noble patriots as we have been universally taught to believe, but a band of hired murderers. Their origin was as follows. It was found by the agitators that the people of Paris could not be goaded to the requisite pitch of bloodthirsty fanaticism ; exasperated by their decency and self-restraint Marat described them as " pitiable revolutionaries." " Give me," he said to Barbaroux, " two hundred Neapolitans armed with daggers, and with them I will overrun France and make a revolution." . . . " Marat's advice was not lost on Barbaroux : he discussed with Monsieur and Madame Roland the advisability of appealing to the South for aid. The result of these deliberations, Barbaroux relates, was a message to Marseilles asking for ' six hundred men who knew how to die—that is to say, six hundred men who knew how to kill ' (p. 251). In the incisive and terrible force of Mrs. Webster's amendment is summed up the whole difference between the actual spirit in which the Revolution was conducted and the glorified conception of its progress and meaning which has been imposed upon us by writers like Carlyle, Morley, Acton, Frederic Harrison and the rest.

One of the cardinal assumptions of the apologists, or rather of the triumphant vindicators of this blood-stained tragedy, is that the Revolution was instrumental in procuring concessions which were otherwise quite unattain-

REVOLUTION AND THE STUDY OF HISTORY 85

able. The idea that the revolutionary leaders were men earnestly striving for reforms and ready to return to the ranks of constitutional and law-abiding citizens when those aims were secured, is not only unsupported by the facts but is in marked contradiction to them. The authorities were ready from the first to make every reasonable concession, but the prospect of peace was again and again frustrated by the action of these same revolutionary leaders. Their most characteristic demands were not genuine but merely made for the purpose of further embarrassing the government, designed in fact to prevent accommodation rather than to secure it. The outbursts of popular fury were not the pardonable result of justifiable indignation against bad government, but the work of dishonest agitators. In short, the contrast between what actually happened and the universally accepted account is so startling that we are not surprised to find Mrs. Webster complaining of the existence of "a conspiracy of history to conceal the facts of the French Revolution." Those, therefore, who appreciate the significance of this denunciation of all hitherto published accounts are naturally impelled to ask : Does such an attempt to conceal the truth exist ? And if so, what is its origin and meaning? If the facts of the French Revolution will not bear the interpretation usually placed upon them, how has it happened .that men of conspicuous attainments, intellectual leaders of their generation in many cases, whose integrity and acumen are above suspicion, should have given to the world so perverse a story.

The reader will be prepared to hear that the explanation of the attitude adopted by all such writers towards the French Revolution lies in what has already been said upon the educational proclivities of historians. The desire to influence conduct is so strong that it amounts to " a conspiracy of history to conceal the facts " in order to encourage what is considered to be a wholesome belief in the entirely retributive nature of revolution.

86 HISTORY AS A SCIENCE

According to this theory, as we have seen, the study of history must be so directed as to support the noblest views of human action, and in particular to confirm the reader in the paths of political virtue. Revolution presents a unique opportunity for the historian to appear in the rôle he loves of political guide and moral teacher, and Carlyle and the rest make the most of it. It is their predetermined opinion that revolution is a dramatic punishment for the wickedness of kings and governments and upper classes, and the French Revolution is regarded by them as a notable instance of this retributive justice. The syllogism put forward for the acceptance of the world has the double merit of simplicity and attractiveness. All revolution is the result of injustice ; the greater the injustice, the more violent the revolution. The French Revolution was very violent, therefore the injustice which preceded and caused it must have been very great. The next step is to enforce this educational lesson by what practically amounts to a dishonest presentation of the facts. However horrible the facts of a revolution may be, the correct attitude is to assume that they are the deeds of beings who are maddened by misgovernment, excesses regrettable indeed, but unavoidable when men undertake the business of " storming the hated citadels of super-stition and injustice."[1]

It is a favourite theme with a certain class of writers that the great cause of the backward condition of the human race is to be found in the spirit of slavish sub-mission which has marked the attitude of the average community towards unjust rulers. All manifestations of a contrary spirit, therefore, deserve enthusiastic encour-agement which is accordingly given in a large-hearted and not too scrutinizing spirit. If the punishment which overwhelms the (by hypothesis) wicked governing classes seems to be characterized by a hideous and indiscriminat-ing fury, rather than directed in accordance with a cal-

[1] Morley's *Miscellanies*, Vol. II, p. 43.

REVOLUTION AND THE STUDY OF HISTORY 87

culated scheme of procedure, that is a detail which does not affect the main issue. A really just and clear-sighted government would so have conducted itself as not to run the risk of incurring popular vengeance, which in the nature of things cannot be very discerning. When wicked kings and governing classes are made to realize that their misdeeds may possibly be punished by September massacres, they will be the more inclined to take heed to their steps and to respect the awful majesty of the sovereign people. Unbiased interpretation of the real meaning of a revolution and of the motives of the chief actors is impossible to historians who commence their investigation under an obsession of this kind. However conscientious in the treatment of their subject they may seem to themselves to be, they are not really examining the facts in the way scientific method requires, but are merely engaged in seeking confirmation of a theory which they definitely held before they had so much as glanced at the evidence before them.

Very different is the method of Mrs. Webster. Having been profoundly impressed by the amazing discrepancy between the obvious significance of certain particular occurrences and the popularly accepted version, she is led to re-examine and to scrutinize all the facts of the French Revolution with a view to discovering what interpretation an unprejudiced authority would place upon them. The result is an overwhelming conviction that the ordinary view is without any real evidence to support it. Yet interesting from the point of view of justice or sentiment as the exposure of an age-long fallacy must always be, there are on the present occasion much more important considerations involved. For in truth, as already pointed out in the opening sentences of this chapter, Mrs. Webster has given us not merely a new view of the French Revolution, not merely a reversal of long-established judgments, which is all that most people see in the book. She has given us a notable instance of

G

HISTORY AS A SCIENCE

the use of the inductive method, and from the conclusions reached we are able to infer what the effect would be if the same procedure were applied not merely to the French Revolution but to the general record of human events. In exposing the " conspiracy of history " with regard to one particular occurrence, Mrs. Webster has dealt a shrewd blow at the educational method in general.

The book, however, has one defect : and those whom nothing would in reality induce to abandon their preconceived idea of what the French Revolution means have seized upon it to belittle the value of the whole work. This defect is the inadequate explanation which the talented authoress offers of those revolutionary phenomena which she so accurately investigates. Nevertheless, paradoxical as it may seem, the insufficiency of Mrs. Webster's explanation leaves the main value of the work entirely unaffected. That value consists, as already pointed out, in the fact that the incidents of the revolution have for the first time in history been dispassionately studied for what they actually are. Thus the first indispensable preliminary of scientific procedure has been amply satisfied. That is the main point. Whatever may be the fate of the hypothesis, the results of the important preliminary investigation in such cases are never rendered useless. It is in this that the superiority of the inductive over the deductive method consists. When writers like Morley and Carlyle approach the subject their treatment of the various incidents is so biased by their antecedent theory that there is nothing of any value left should their theory be upset, and all has to be done over again by the investigator who next takes up the problem. When, however, an inquirer allows the facts to speak for themselves and to suggest a theory in the proper scientific manner instead of imposing a theory upon the facts, then even if the theory is not accepted, the facts remain, all honestly spread out, as it were, in the Thucydidean manner for the use of future observers.

REVOLUTION AND THE STUDY OF HISTORY 89

Darwin's theory of Coral Reefs is incorrect and his account of the Origin of Species is insufficient. But the value of his preliminary observation and array of facts is permanent : and his name will ever be honoured because his method entitled him to success even if he may not happen to have attained it in the fullest measure. Similarly, the main value of Mrs. Webster's work will remain unimpaired whatever happens to her conclusions.

Mrs. Webster traces the Revolution to four main causes : (1) The Orleanist conspiracy. (2) The conspiracy of the Illuminati. (3) The intrigues of Prussia. (4) The intrigues of the English revolutionaries.

It is true that all these agencies have been unduly neglected because they tend to give the Revolution a vulgar aspect, to weaken the impressiveness of its teaching, and to rob it of those ennobling truths which educational historians are determined to extract from the subject. It is right, therefore, that these four causes should receive the attention which they deserve. Nevertheless, when all has been said, they must probably be regarded as secondary and not as primary causes. The machinations of the sect of Illuminati in particular, carefully organized and universally extended as they were, are made accountable for more than they will really bear. Certain revolutionary ideas and aphorisms for instance, and certain methods of producing disturbance and anarchy, are perhaps correctly attributed to the definite instructions of agents of the Illuminati. But the impression is left that if it had not been for such definite instructions, anarchy would not have supervened nor would the disturbances have been provoked. The truth is, however, that these ideas and aphorisms are as old as the phenomenon of revolution itself and are such as naturally suggest themselves to certain depraved or fanatical dispositions in times of political disturbance.

A perusal of sections 82 to 84 of the third book of Thucydides, where he gives an account of the revolution

HISTORY AS A SCIENCE

in Corcyra, will go far to prove to the reader that the symptoms of which we are speaking had their parallel in the earliest times, and are nothing more nor less than phenomena of all human nature under conditions of anarchy. Under such circumstances in the words of Thucydides " human nature shows itself ungoverned in passion, above respect for justice, *and the enemy of all superiority.*" Similarly, a precept such as that of St. Etienne, "everything must be destroyed, since every-thing must be re-made," does not need to be explained as the outcome of the suggestion of certain definite individuals among the Illuminati, but is the very essence of the revolutionary idea at all times and places : while as to the actual methods employed the same or some-thing very like them would have been discussed and put in force if the sect of the Illuminati had never existed at all.

A similar criticism may be passed with regard to the other causes assigned. Previous historians intent upon proving that the French were a " nation of slaves brought by long years of oppression to a pitch of exasperation which found a vent in the crimes and horrors of the Revolution " have no doubt very greatly underrated the importance of the Orleanistic conspiracy, not merely as a cause of the original outbreak, but as an active influence throughout a large part of the Revolution itself. But it is possible that too much weight has been laid upon what as far as it goes is a " vera causa." Again, with regard to German intrigues, it is impossible to deny that " There was thus a double strain of German influence at work behind the French Revolution—the political and philosophical. The first inspired by Frederick the Great and carried out by Von der Goltz ; the second inspired by Weishaupt and conducted by Anacharis Clootz, the Prussian sent to France for the purpose." Though Mira-beau and the others no doubt found both the philosoph-ical and political assistance of the Germans very useful,

REVOLUTION AND THE STUDY OF HISTORY 91

the forces of anarchy would have pursued their fatal course without any such external stimulus. When once the mob has felt its power, fanatical or bloodthirsty agitators appear like magic with their wild or infamous suggestions, and urge it to fresh mischief. All the phenomena of the French Revolution, down to the minutest details, are explicable on general principles without having recourse to the theory that the revolutionary leaders were deliberately instructed in revolutionary methods and ideas.

In spite of all this, however, in spite of the fact that we cannot accept the hypothesis suggested in explanation of the facts which are so fearlessly and faithfully recorded, Mrs. Webster's book is likely to remain " a permanent acquisition."[1] To abandon the popular educational point of view in favour of the strict investigation of the facts is to carry out the principles which the great master, Thucydides, laid down.

It will be readily perceived that it is not merely the theory of history which is benefited by the inductive method. It is valuable also as an aid to political practice. A study of the dread symptoms of incipient anarchy, and of the way in which human beings are prone to act under revolutionary conditions, is above all things desirable. Governments at the present time especially must have as full a knowledge as possible of the psychological disorders which may affect those for whom they are called upon to prescribe. They should be able to recognize the characteristic features which mark the approach of so fatal a disease as anarchy so that they may be able to take their preventive measures in the right way and at the right time. What is most required is, of course, a knowledge of the truth. But the educational method of studying revolution to which we have been hitherto accustomed is almost deliberately designed to conceal the truth, in the endeavour to give such a colour to the facts as shall

[1] κτῆμα ἐς ἀεί.

HISTORY AS A SCIENCE

conduce to the moral and political edification rather than to the information of mankind. In pursuance of this design historians by a sort of tacit convention when dealing with any political differences between a people and its rulers, almost always assume the people to be right and the rulers to be wrong. History is filled with examples of this inveterate habit ; but if a particular instance is required we may cite a dictum of Sully which Morley in his *Life of Burke* says " practical politicians and political students should bind about their neck " so profoundly valuable does he consider it to be. " The populace never rebels from a passion for attack but from impatience of suffering." It was precisely because Louis XVI endeavoured to deal with the political crisis with which he was confronted in this spirit and with these preconceptions, that the Revolution gradually gathered its terrible momentum. It is because historians have approached the study of the Revolution in this spirit and with these preconceptions that they have missed its real significance, and have adopted an interpretation of events as perverse and misleading as that which has been described.

We may admit that no disturbance would have taken place if the history of France had been more fortunate and its government more capable and efficient. But this is a very different thing from asserting or implying as most writers do that the fury of the French people gives the measure of their sufferings. Observation reveals the fact that the atrocities which follow the overthrow of a central authority have no necessary connection with the remembrance of previous wrongs and afford no reliable indication of the political or social injustice to which the people have been subjected. Such a view, however, is profoundly distasteful to writers who resent being deprived of any opportunity for an impressive political exhortation. According to Lord Morley, the Revolution was " the final explosion of a fabric under

REVOLUTION AND THE STUDY OF HISTORY 93

which every yard had been mined by the long endeavour for half a century of an army of destroyers deliberate and involuntary, direct and oblique, such as the world has never at any other time beheld." [1]   Or again, its fury is attributed to the activities of certain baleful beings in their " far resounding fiery workshops where a hundred hands wrought the cunning implements and Cyclopean engines that were to serve in storming the hated citadels of superstition and injustice." [2]

These grandiloquent utterances show us the educational method in its most misleading form, since we now know that the outbreak itself was preventable, and that with just a little more firmness and a little more luck at the beginning the necessary reforms might have been introduced without any revolution at all.   For it has been placed beyond a doubt that neither the spirit which gave rise to the outbreaks, nor the malignity which inspired its worst episodes, was the genuine expression of discontent.   The chief characteristic, even of the opening stages of the Revolution, is not the single-hearted determination to get the sufferings of the people relieved but the systematic attempt to " create grievances in order to exploit them."   The most distinctive and terrible features of a revolution have nothing whatever to do with " impatience of suffering," as Sully and Morley, and as we shall presently see Mr. Lloyd George, insist, but are due to an entirely different and more sinister cause, which the scientific historian must examine with all the greater care because philanthropists and educational historians have entirely ignored it.

There is nothing mysterious about the problem. Inductive study leaves no room for doubt that the phenomena of revolution are nothing else than the phenomena of human nature when released from political control. At the consequences which ensue we have already inci-

[1] Morley's *Miscellanies*, Vol. II, p. 41.
[2] *Ibid.*, p. 43.

94 HISTORY AS A SCIENCE

dentally glanced. A revolution has three phases. In the first place, the control of affairs falls into the hands of leaders who are for the most part unpractical visionaries utterly incapable of dealing with a crisis which could only be successfully surmounted by strong governmental authority combined with a wide governmental experience. Under their management the disorder is increased until affairs are beyond their control, and the second phase supervenes. Then the worst passions of human nature are let loose and indulged, at first under the pretext of zeal for the State and afterwards without any pretext at all. The chaos into which government falls and the consequent weakening of its repressive powers speedily brings about the last phase of revolution, which is nothing else than the victory of the bad over the good. Though it is not fair to say, as one writer does, that revolution from first to last consists of nothing but an unjustifiable attempt on the part of those who are deservedly lowest to displace those who are deservedly highest, that is undoubtedly what happens if it is allowed to run its course. Unless firmness is exerted at the outset a movement which may have had its first tentative beginnings in a justifiable desire for reform ends in a carnival of bloodshed.

To provide against such an eventuality is the most important duty which statesmanship owes to civilization, and it is the function of history to assist in this task. From what has been said it will be plain that statesmen would be helpless in a time of emergency if they were compelled to rely upon the type of history which regards as a necessary process of recuperation what is in reality a dangerous disease. While the so-called curative effects of a revolution, such as they are, can be secured at infinitely smaller cost, the political and moral damage is almost beyond calculation.

What treatment, then, it will be asked, should follow the correct diagnosis of the revolutionary malady? As

REVOLUTION AND THE STUDY OF HISTORY 95

we have seen, the sentimentalist approaches the problem under the idea that revolutionary excesses are the result of long-continued denial of the just demands of the people. Upon this assumption the only proper way to meet revolution is by concession. Since the popular clamour and violence is by hypothesis entirely due to political injustice, it will cease upon the granting of reforms. This theory finds no support in the history of the French or any other revolution. " Every concession made by the King to the desires of the people, every step in the work of reform, was the signal for a fresh outbreak of revolutionary fury."[1] Even in the case of Madame Roland who has hitherto been held up as a noble and single-hearted worker for a good cause, it is clearly shown that she did her utmost to foster this fatal spirit of discontent. To such a degree was this obstinate disaffection and irreconcilable animosity carried that as the Revolution proceeded, the leaders, not satisfied with rejecting all idea of accommodation, harboured the further design of bringing to the scaffold all those who exhibited a more reasonable spirit. " It was not a case of misdirected popular fury but of a definite system pursued by agitators, which consisted in exterminating everyone who encouraged contentment with the old Regime."[2] In this way and in accordance with what, as will be presently pointed out, seems to be a psychological law, all ideas of reasonable accommodation finally disappear, passions become more unrestrained, political desires more violent and chimerical, until those who like Madame Roland were at one time leaders in revolutionary extravagance are put to death because they fail to satisfy the very passions which they have excited. It is this insatiability of expectation which is one of the most characteristic features of revolution ; and it demands especial study.

We seem, in fact, to be witnessing the perversion of an originally useful motive, a motive which, when

---

[1] Mrs. Webster's *French Revolution*, p. 98.　　[2] *Ibid.*, p. 113.

96 HISTORY AS A SCIENCE

restrained within due limits, has been of much value to the human race. Aristotle, it may be remembered, attributes the rise of civilization to the fact that " man not only wishes to live but to live well." This law of " progressive desire "[1] as it has been aptly called, is exaggerated in times of revolution until it touches the borderland of madness, and becomes an insane belief in the possibility of the immediate realization of a political heaven on earth. The loss of intellectual balance thus creates an atmosphere the very opposite of that which is necessary for the initiation of reasonable changes. Nor is this peculiar frenzy characteristic only of ignorant natures, but may affect even sedate philosophers who have made a special study of social questions. It is thus that we must account for the strange and unexpected developments in the character of such a thinker as Condorcet. Less than two years after he talked about " attachment to the forms of monarchy and respect for the royal person and prerogative " he became " an ardent republican ; and in less than twelve months after that he had voted the guilt of the King."[2] It is this insatiability of desire and not Lord Morley's " impatience of suffering " which urges the revolutionary from one extravagant demand to another ; until the wholesale destruction of the existing framework of society is regarded as necessary for the salvation of the people, and a condition of things ensues under which the lowest and most ferocious of the community get matters into their own hands. The spirit of murder, masquerading at first as the embodiment of stern political justice, slakes its thirst for blood under the pretext of removing the enemies of the State, but soon begins to enjoy a carnage for its own sake alone. Finally a terrible suspicion assails the agitators that their own methods will be employed against

[1] An answer given by a lady pupil to Professor Bonamy Price, which greatly delighted him.

[2] Morley's *Miscellanies*, Vol. II, p. 191.

REVOLUTION AND THE STUDY OF HISTORY 97

themselves, and the whole movement becomes a horrible game in which the aim is to murder any possible adversary before he has time to murder you. Whoever stops half-way in a revolution, as St. Just said, digs his own grave.

As for the will of the people, it is recognized now that it is never heard and never can be heard in a revolution. The views which prevail are those of the partially deranged minority whose aim it is to prevent the opinion of the reasonable majority from being attended to. Only under strong government can the opinion of the sane-minded have their proper weight. " The only deputations recognized as representative of the poeple are those organized by revolutionary leaders and marching at the word of command, spontaneous demonstrations are inevitably silenced and declared seditious."[1] " Altogether no less than sixty departments had risen against the tyranny of the Convention." Such was the attitude of the twenty-five millions of France who, according to Carlyle, looked to the " Mountain " for salvation.[2]

Just as the discontent before the Revolution is depicted in the gloomiest colours in order to account for the violence of the upheaval, so the gains of France after the Revolution are exaggerated in order to prove that this period of bloody anarchy produced ennobling results which could not otherwise have been obtained. Thus, in addition to " cooking " the evidence, so to speak, in order to show that poor Louis XVI got no more than he and his ancestors deserved, the educational method takes care to advertise a long list of blessings to which the Revolution is supposed to have given rise. Those, however, who, approaching the subject with an open mind and are under no obligation to prove either its retributive or its corrective nature, find it hard to identify either the spiritual advantages which it brought to France, or the

---

[1] Mrs. Webster's *French Revolution*, pp. 215, 216.
[2] *Ibid.*, p. 405.

HISTORY AS A SCIENCE

moral uplift which it is supposed to have given to Europe and even the whole world.

England certainly had no political lessons to learn from it. Any trace of good in the political ideas of pre-revolutionary France were borrowed from England, and spoilt in the process of carrying them into practice. All that the Revolution did for England was unnecessarily to disturb the current of our political life and to throw back reform for forty years. The fable of its marvellous and far-reaching influence upon the human mind and upon the political prospects of the human race is the inevitable corollary of the unproved educational assumptions as to its real significance and origin.

We have found, then, that a study of the French Revolution on inductive principles shows that though it was in a certain sense, and to a certain extent, the consequence of previous misgovernment, it was not the inevitable consequence of such misgovernment. Though France was politically and economically in a thoroughly bad condition, it was not, as most historians would have us believe, past all cure except that of such a revolution as actually did take place. We have seen reason to conclude also that if the Revolution was to a large extent precipitated and encouraged by the Orleanist intrigue and the devilish cunning of the Prussian government, yet it is unnecessary to attribute the insane hatred of authority, the bloody factions, the ruinous anarchy which marked its subsequent course, to " a combination of conspiracies." These terrible consequences are inherent in the psychology of the masses when by the removal of a political control they have been reduced to a condition under which the bad have a natural advantage over the good. If the Government is destroyed and nothing effective put in its place, the rest follows as a matter of course, and would follow under these conditions in any country in the world.

What then, it will be asked, is the chief lesson which

REVOLUTION AND THE STUDY OF HISTORY 99

a scientific study of the phenomena of revolution would suggest ? The most important lesson is at the same time one of extreme simplicity. Looking at the matter from a practical point of view, the occurrence of the French Revolution, with all the horrors which it brought in its train, was merely due to unpreparedness. When we rid ourselves of those exaggerated ideas of dramatic retribution, carefully worked up by educational historians in order to enhance the solemnity of their lesson, and while not forgetting the existence of predisposing causes both from the political and philosophical point of view, study the immediate reasons of its outbreak, we find that it began and followed its terrible course because the ruling authorities were ignorant of the nature of the phenomenon with which they had to deal. " The old Regime, resolutely blind to the coming danger, allowed itself to be destroyed without striking a blow in self-defence." Ignorance of the fatal nature of the revolutionary disease and a consequent inability to take the proper measures to meet it was the cause of the destruction of the French monarchy and of all that followed. The Government failed to cope with the situation chiefly in consequence of that humanitarian attitude which radicals and socialists assure us is the only method of pacifying political discontent. Those in authority acted on the assumption that since turbulence is solely due to " impatience of suffering," it will immediately subside when measures of reform are taken ; and that the excellence of governmental intentions will be duly recognized and appreciated by a discerning and grateful people. They were unacquainted with the psychological law, as it may be called, in accordance with which fanatical or dishonest agitators immediately manufacture fresh grievances as fast as the old ones are removed, and keep discontent alive by putting forward schemes which even if honest are impossible of fulfilment, because they have no real relation to the actualities of human nature and

HISTORY AS A SCIENCE

the possibilities of political life. The governmental authorities were from the first at a disadvantage, not because they were harsh and wicked, but because they were well-intentioned, and because their opponents knew from the first that they were unlikely to take preventive measures of adequate severity. This kindliness of feeling, this disinclination on the part of a government to proceed to extremities, is an honourable feature of human nature upon which the advocates of " direct action " have always relied. As the great Mirabeau explained to his disreputable associates : " You have nothing to fear from the aristocrats : these people do not pillage, they do not burn, they do not assassinate." That is the calculation which always emboldens revolt, and Mirabeau might well have added on his own behalf and on behalf of revolutionaries in general, " we do all these things and in this lies our strength and our assurance of victory."

Perhaps it will be said that all such warnings are unnecessary at the present day, and that after the events in Russia no sane man can be under any delusion as to the real significance of the savage excesses of revolution. Unfortunately this reasonable anticipation seems still very far from fulfilment. No less a person than Mr. Lloyd George has seen fit to encourage the hypocritical complaisance towards revolutionary crime which radicals and socialists so frequently adopt. " There is no savagery," he said, while apologizing for the Russian horrors, " like that of a trustful people who have been imposed upon." [1] The Grand Duchess Elizabeth, regarded by those who knew her as the most kind-hearted and saintly woman in Europe, a ministering angel to all who were in distress, daughter of our beloved Princess Alice, was beaten to death by the butt-end of rifles on the night of July 17th, 1918, and thrown into a mine shaft ; presumably for the purpose of warning the world

[1] *Daily Chronicle*, December, 1923.

REVOLUTION AND THE STUDY OF HISTORY 101

that a trustful people must not be too greatly imposed upon.

No discussion of revolutionary symptoms and their treatment would be complete without some reference to a feature of the French political constitution which was not only largely answerable for letting the revolutionary movement get beyond control, but also for the fact that there was any revolutionary movement at all. The great defect of the French constitution is usually supposed to have been that it was not representative, that is to say, that it did not provide for the association of the people with the government. But an even greater weakness is to be found in the fact that it did not provide for the presence of intellect in the executive. As we have seen in a previous chapter, historians, in their educational capacity, ignore the importance of intellect in government, because it is not a theme upon which an impressive lesson can be preached. As a consequence misgovernment, except in certain glaring instances, is almost invariably traced by them to moral rather than to intellectual causes. Though they are agreed that the ultimate reason of the troubles from which France suffered is to be ascribed in a last analysis to autocracy, nevertheless in consequence of their political obsessions they fail to perceive that in addition to preventing the people from enjoying the right of self-government autocracy has the coincident disadvantage of preventing the people from enjoying the right of government by the highest available talent. Concerned merely to find confirmation for the conventional belief that the differences between good and bad government is merely the difference between absolute government and government by the will of the people, they miss the vital fact that absolute government prevents the systematic rise and employment of able statesmen, and that it was from the want of able statesmanship that France was chiefly suffering both before and during the Revolution. As

HISTORY AS A SCIENCE

the value of ability in government has been fully discussed by the writer elsewhere, it is unnecessary to say more in the present place upon the general aspect of the question. What more particularly concerns us here is the disastrous effect of unintelligence at the outbreak of the revolutionary movement.

Mrs. Webster rightly points out that the loss of Mirabeau by the Court party was one of the greatest calamities.[1] " The letter of Mirabeau was ignored, his memoirs never reached the King, and all the disasters he had foreseen came to pass. So the man who might have saved the monarchy, smarting at this rebuff, threw himself into the opposite camp, and devoted all his force, his eloquence and his vast energy to overthrow the government." The loss of one Mirabeau was bad enough. But the absence of a system of government such as existed in England undoubtedly meant the loss of many such men. Had superior ability been tacitly recognized as one of the main qualifications for the exercise of political power, not only would the assistance of Mirabeau have been instantly accepted, but similar men might, or rather undoubtedly would, have been available in the hour of danger. The best equipment for a statesman who has to face a revolution is not a high moral character or love of justice, still less fervent attachment to democratic principles, but a capacity for seeing what to do and what not to do. In so far as the revolution had anything retributive about it, more than anything else it was a retribution for the denial of the free career to political talent. As the present writer has elsewhere pointed out,[2] if the administration from the time of Richelieu had been modelled on the English fashion, so as to utilize the services of the ablest members of the French aristocracy, there would never have been any thought of revolution. And even as things were, had

[1] Mrs. Webster's *French Revolution*, pp. 14, 15.
[2] *Government by Natural Selection.*

REVOLUTION AND THE STUDY OF HISTORY 103

there been, as late as the year 1788, men capable of taking the direction of affairs out of the hands of the well-meaning but incompetent Louis XVI, the French nation would have been saved even at the eleventh hour.

Yet granting that we presuppose in government the requisite knowledge and intelligence, the method of dealing with threatened revolution would seem to present a very serious problem. The main difficulty with which democratic governors are confronted when attempts are being made to overthrow the constitution consists in this, that while it is imperative that order should be maintained, there is a strong prejudice against what is apparently the only means of restraining anarchy, the employment of the military. Indeed, such employment is not only unpopular but inefficient. The army being, to a large extent, drawn from the same class as the revolutionists is peculiarly open to the suggestion that to use force against those who are their friends and comrades is an act of the basest treachery, particularly when those friends are represented as engaged in securing justice. The fate of France was sealed when under the influence of revolutionary propaganda the army went over to the mutineers, and the guardians of order became the abettors of anarchy. Clearly, therefore, those who wish to prevent the outbreak of revolution are under the necessity of finding some substitute for the use of the military.

Fortunately, as recent events have shown, this difficulty can be overcome if the government is sufficiently alert to mark the first symptoms of revolution and to take its measures accordingly. When the executive is aware of the true meaning of revolution, and is prepared to bring a little common sense to bear upon the situation, a little special preparation is all that is needed for the protection of society.

At the moment of the greatest revolutionary danger

HISTORY AS A SCIENCE

there exists in every country a number of individuals all ready, of their own free will and from the highest motives, to perform duties which can no longer be adequately performed by a sorely tried administration. Their success is certain provided only they are organized. A revolution of the kind of which we are speaking is never the work of the people as a whole, but only of a violent minority. Even at the height of such revolutionary fury as was witnessed in France or Russia it may be taken for certain that, in spite of the fact that many decent citizens are led astray by visionary promises or are paralysed by fear, those who remain well-affected to the State are always superior in numbers to those who wish for its destruction or violent alteration. Nothing more is needed to prevent revolution, if it is merely in its incipient stage, or to arrest it if it has progressed further, than to call upon these individuals to come forward in defence of law and order. Hitherto these vast reserves of strength, amply sufficient to preserve the health and safety of the constitution, have been wasted ; the peace-loving, law-abiding majority have sat with idle hands because, owing to ignorance of what revolution really means, they have never anticipated that any necessity would ever arise for calling on them to undertake their own defence and that of the State. When once they are made to understand the necessity for action their power is irresistible. To summon all right-minded citizens to come forward in defence of law and order is the simple and effective method of preventing revolution.

In order to make this clear it is necessary to consider what was the condition of things before this method of meeting incipient revolution was adopted. In all European countries, until recent times, the initial advantage has always been in the hands of the revolutionists, because they have been ready on the instant to appeal to force, while the law-abiding members of the com-

REVOLUTION AND THE STUDY OF HISTORY 105

munity, in consequence of their life-long tradition and training, regard the use of force otherwise than through the agency of the government as an unthinkable procedure. They may not take the law into their own hands, as the phrase goes ; in other words, they are forbidden to defend themselves. Under these circumstances the very virtues of the law-abiding citizen are his undoing. The greater his respect for the decencies of political procedure, the easier is the victory of his opponents who are deterred by no such scruples. Thus the odds are from the first in favour of the party of disorder, because they are able, as it were, to mobilize on the instant, while the well-affected having previously handed over their right of self-protection to a government which is paralysed when the time for action arrives, continue to rely upon the safeguard of the law which is no longer of any use.

Happily we have had evidence that the old habit of hesitancy and inaction in the face of threatened danger from a violent popular outbreak is over, and that the necessity of reinforcing the ordinary processes of law by other methods in times of internal crisis is now recognized as one of the duties of government. All the world complimented the British Government and people upon the way in which they met the General Strike of 1926. Unfortunately preventive measures by their very success are apt to destroy the evidence of their necessity. " The ill that's done you can compute, but rarely what's prevented." Those who by wise action save the nation from disaster deprive themselves of the means of proving that disaster would have ensued unless precautionary measures had been taken. Accordingly we are now earnestly assured by the socialists that the General Strike was purely economic, and that to regard it as the preliminary to revolution is merely bourgeois malignity. It is as well, therefore, to recall the fact that the French Revolution was precipitated because Louis XVI believed

HISTORY AS A SCIENCE

in the honesty of similarly hypocritical indignation. The very best way to render revolution inevitable is to adopt this attitude of simple-minded reliance upon the goodness of revolutionary human nature. Granting that some of those who initiate a revolt make their assurances of moderation in all good faith, yet one of the most pronounced features of all revolution is the utter inability of the original promoters to control the movement when once it has been started. As soon as the rising has become fully developed, the Kerenskys and MacDonalds and Cooks are thrust aside, and a tyranny of murderers masquerading as the agents of the will of the people is presently inaugurated. The psychology of the crowd is now sufficiently well known to make it certain that any rising which aims at the overthrow of the constitution would speedily degenerate into a carnival of crime if allowed to take its course unhampered.

There are many, however, who, while under no illusion as to the real meaning of revolution, believe that it is impossible in England, because the lower orders are more just and fair-minded than those of any other nation, and we may therefore trust them to perceive that whatever the faults of the administration for the last two hundred years it has done nothing to deserve a fate such as that which in the opinion of our English Bolshevists was so justly meted out to the Bourbons and the Romanoffs and their adherents. Such an argument is based on the old unfounded assumption that the atrocities of a revolution are committed in revenge for previous injustices; and it is therefore entirely worthless. Though the English character, we may hope, has rather more self-restraint than that of contemporary nations, close observers have detected an underlying element of savagery which, if once it got out of control, would produce results not conspicuously different from those which have been produced elsewhere under revolutionary conditions. We have therefore no

REVOLUTION AND THE STUDY OF HISTORY 107

valid reason for assuming that the quality of mercy would be more pronounced in an English revolution than in any other ; as Professor Hearnshaw has pointed out the " Trades Disputes Act of 1906 and the Trades Union Act of 1913 have delivered constitutional working men into the merciless hands of the terrorist and the exploiter, the bully and the blackmailer, the peaceful picketer and the political levier."[1] The ways of the peaceful picketer under the reign of law are sufficient indication of what would happen if ordinary governmental restraints were withdrawn.

There is, however, a further contingency suggested by the inductive study of revolutionary phenomena for which a wise nation should be prepared. In the recent crisis of the General Strike we had a government sane and courageous enough to take the requisite measures for ensuring the national supplies and for suppressing open violence. Unfortunately with the spread of communistic influence, for socialism in theory inevitably becomes communism in practice, conditions may arise in which it is not possible to count with certainty upon the continuance of governmental sanity and courage, and when attempts to carry into practice the wild notions of the fanatics may sweep away the ordinary safeguards of civilized life. Under these circumstances no other course is left for the order-loving classes except to combine for the purpose of performing for themselves those legitimate functions which government is no longer able or willing to perform for them. Government from one point of view may be regarded as a device for relieving the citizen of a duty which he would otherwise have to perform on his own behalf, that of self-defence. If government fails to fulfil the contract which it has undertaken in this respect, then there is nothing left except for the citizen to perform it for himself. It is this consideration which raises the action of Signor Mus-

[1] *Morning Post*, April 30, 1924.

108 HISTORY AS A SCIENCE

solini far above that of any ordinary dictator, and gives it a world-significance. Mirabeau, it will be remembered, bade his associates take courage from the fact that there was nothing to be feared from the upper classes in the way of reprisals, and this has always been a secret source of satisfaction to revolutionaries. " Why don't you revolt ? " said Mr. Tom Mann ; " are you afraid of Scotland Yard ? " Here the belief is clearly implied that when an inadequate police force has been disposed of, the upper classes would not have the energy or courage to defend themselves. There can be no question that this anticipation has long been one of the main incentives to revolutionary violence, and we owe to Signor Mussolini and his Fascists the revelation of an effectual method of correcting this impression. They have taught the world that if there is no other way of preserving law and order the method of revolutionaries can be turned against themselves with superior effect. They have demonstrated the fact that direct action is a game that the upper classes, that is to say, the law-abiding classes, can play if they are forced to it, even better than their attackers, and this is perhaps the most salutary political lesson that the world has learned in a thousand years. For it means nothing less than this, that if the ordinary citizen has sufficient imagination to realize his strength, and sufficient energy to use it, no attack upon the constitution has the slightest chance of being successful. Nothing could be better calculated to temper with discretion the zeal of future revolutionaries than an appreciation of the fact that they can no longer count, with Mirabeau, on having to deal with a helpless flock of law-abiding sheep, but will be confronted by men even more resolute and determined than themselves.

The time has now come when clear-minded patriots should denounce the one-sided constitutionalism which prevents those who wish to preserve the State from

REVOLUTION AND THE STUDY OF HISTORY 109

adopting a course of action which is permitted to those who wish to destroy it. The law should no longer be allowed to paralyse its own defenders, in spite of the indignation of the radicals and socialists who seem to think that the order-loving classes in Italy were guilty of an unspeakable crime when they declined to allow themselves to be plundered and murdered any longer in the sacred name of liberty. It is the old story, " *cet animal est méchant, quand on l'attaque il se defend.*" It is clear that the Fascists saved Italy from ruin ; but some authorities are uneasy because as *The Times* says : " it was saved by violence and by an open disregard of constitutional rights and forms." Those who argue in this way entirely miss the real point at issue. To insist in revolutionary times upon a strictly legal procedure is to give the lawless the overwhelming advantage which has already been pointed out. It is as if one portion of the community were allowed to go about with loaded weapons ready to open fire instantaneously and without provocation, while their unhappy victims are forbidden to pull a trigger in self-defence until they had received the belated permission of a court of law.

It is possible that the English people may never be forced to imitate the Italians, but it is not wise to assume that this is certain. Indeed it is because we have already shown ourselves apt pupils that we have been able to repress the forces of anarchy. There can, in fact, be little doubt that the work done by the British Fascisti in the two or three years before the General Strike, though it was unrecognized by the government, and unacknowledged by the nation, had a decisive influence upon the course of events. Their existence was useful in more ways than one. They forced the government to recognize the fact that if adequate measures were not officially taken to anticipate revolution, they would be taken unofficially. They familiarized a large portion of the community with the idea that they might some

HISTORY AS A SCIENCE

day be called upon to organize their own defence, and but for this warning the special constables and transport helpers who were for the most part Fascisti, giving their services anonymously, would not have been forthcoming in such numbers and with such readiness. In fact, without both their physical and moral support the governmental measures might have failed ; as it is, the world has learned the lesson that violent revolution need never take place again in the history of any resolute and self-respecting nation, if the loyal portion of the community are ready to take measures for their own defence, with or without the assistance of government.

CHAPTER VI

THE STUDY OF HISTORY FROM THE POINT OF VIEW OF CONDUCT

WE have seen that the serious study of history may be approached from two points of view, either for the purpose of increasing knowledge or for the purpose of assisting conduct.[1] While the subject of the preceding chapters has been the prejudice which has been caused to the scientific study of history by the intrusion of a too absorbing interest in the political and moral welfare of mankind, the subject of the present chapter will be the reverse of this, the prejudice which may be caused to morality if we allow certain inductively justified conclusions to influence conduct. Whereas formerly the attainment of scientific results was the only consideration, it is the moral point of view that is now all-important. In short, when we are dealing with the practical aspects of life, the educational motive which has been consistently denounced in the previous pages must be taken into the fullest consideration. And the reason for this is that the study of history reveals the existence of certain natural tendencies which, though useful at an earlier stage of social evolution, eventually offend the developed moral instinct of civilized man. The science and the art of human affairs must be kept distinct.

The remarkable difference between the science of his-

[1] The fact that history may be legitimately used merely for the purpose of picturesque and brilliant narrative need not concern us here.

HISTORY AS A SCIENCE

tory and other sciences may be illustrated in the following way. Generally speaking, man is able to turn his scientific investigations to account by imitating the processes of nature which he studies, with such alterations as may suit his particular purpose. His powers are thus enriched in manifold ways by a study of nature's laws. It might therefore have been anticipated that observation of the principles of social and political evolution as revealed by the scientific study of history would have put the statesman in possession of truths which could be directly utilized. Yet, as it happens, knowledge of the laws of political and social evolution, though unquestionably necessary for assisting the progress of the human race, cannot be utilized by way of direct imitation, because only part of the information gained by the study of history is consonant with a respect for moral principles. It is this intrusion of moral considerations which entirely differentiates the science of history from other sciences. As a writer quoted in another work points out : " nature uses evil as the raw material of good." Not all the lessons of history are fit for imitation. In the process of social and political evolution methods may be discerned in operation which contribute to the progress of mankind, but which man, the subject of that solicitude, condemns.

As it happens, the distinction between the art and science of politics, which may seem to the reader laboured, unsound and paradoxical, has received a remarkable illustration in the life and writings of a celebrated man. There was, in fact, one historian who ventured once upon a time not only to study political phenomena from the scientific point of view, but to suggest in a famous work that the lessons of history were directly convertible into political practice ; and the universal opprobrium which has overwhelmed his name affords a striking illustration of the strength of the moral feeling which forbids the imitation of political precedents unless they

FROM THE POINT OF VIEW OF CONDUCT 113

accord with the moral law. So great, indeed, has been the antipathy aroused by the precepts laid down by Machiavelli[1] in *The Prince,* that the true significance of this work has never been really apprehended even up to the present day. Almost every sort of motive has been attributed to him but the right one, and his whole procedure has been represented in an entirely false light.

The generally accepted theory, in spite of the many indications which show it to be incorrect, is that Machiavelli's mind had become so warped by the degrading nature of the political atmosphere by which he was surrounded that he had lost all sense of the difference between right and wrong. Though we may admit in all Italians of his time a lower moral standpoint than that of a later civilization, the real explanation of his action is very different. Perceiving that the benefits which science had already conferred upon the world in his day were due to the use of the inductive method, Machiavelli conceived the idea of applying the same method to the study of history. He thought that history should be placed upon the same basis as the physical sciences, and that a similar use should be made of the results obtained. His object was to discover some means of rehabilitating a country which, distracted by internal dissensions, had become the sport of foreign powers. History was therefore to be examined in order to discover how national confusion might be converted into national order, and how a people hopelessly divided against itself might be enabled to present a united front to its foes. In such an investigation, according to Machiavelli's point of view, the question of morality did not arise. If the procedure was to be strictly scientific he argued with a ruthless but unanswerable logic that a natural and not a moral sanction was all that was required.

[1] The view of Machiavelli here taken was published by the present writer as far back as 1888.

114 HISTORY AS A SCIENCE

To an intellect such as that of Machiavelli surveying history to discover by what methods internal dissensions have most frequently been cured the answer could not long be in doubt. Learning from his inductive survey that "usurpation" has been one of the most frequent and effective means of national regeneration, he took a step which, on scientific grounds, he was not only justified in taking but was bound to take. He urged that those methods which past history had shown to be effective in bringing about political unity should be adopted with the view of bringing to an end those internecine quarrels of republican Italy which left her a helpless prey to the foreigner. Only by union would his beloved country be enabled to resist the successive invasions of French, German and Spanish marauders who were destroying its very soul, and be made strong enough to take its rightful place among the nations of the world.

If History is consulted on a point like this, its verdict is certain.[1] There is only one cure for a condition of political anarchy such as was then draining the life-blood of Italy, and that is strong central government. The desperate hostility which animated the various Italian republics is, as a rule, lightly explained on the ground that "they abused their freedom"; by which two things are apparently implied; firstly, that republican institutions are naturally conducive to amicable international relations; and secondly, that the moral development of the Italians was sufficiently high to enable them to profit by whatever advantages a republican form of government may possess.

Machiavelli knew both these assumptions to be incorrect. His study of history, especially we may suppose of Greek history, had revealed to him the truth that the hostility of the Italian states did not come about because they abused their freedom, but because they used it. It was the natural, not the abnormal,

[1] See the present writer's *Origin of Government*.

FROM THE POINT OF VIEW OF CONDUCT 115

result of the conditions in which they were placed. He saw that under such circumstances republics, even if they are of the same nationality, are always in a more or less desperate condition of rivalry; that permanent co-operation for great national ends is out of the question; and that they can be prevented from making continual war upon one another by forcible means alone. He also knew that the moral defects of his countrymen were increased, not lessened, by the liberty they enjoyed. In short, Machiavelli, being free from any *a priori* convictions as to the necessary beauty of republican institutions, and having before his eyes the fearful object-lesson of his distracted country, urged Lorenzo to carry into practice the means by which, as inductive observation showed him, such a state of things had been remedied in the past. His whole offence was the belief that the historical investigator, like his counterpart in physics, may be allowed to utilize the information he has wrested from nature. Of Machiavelli it may be truly said that the correctness of his scientific procedure is the measure of his guilt.

Yet the significance of the fact that Machiavelli produced historical precedent, that is to say, from the point of view which we are emphasizing, scientific warrant, for the course which he proposed, is entirely overlooked by critics of philosophic repute like Lord Morley. Lord Morley's pronouncement on the subject is, indeed, generally regarded as decisive. Yet though his essay is pervaded with that air of complete finality which radical writers know so well how to impart to all their principles and prejudices, there is, as we shall presently see, not the faintest appreciation of the real question at issue.

There are three real points in Machiavelli's argument. The first is that the licence of the separate Italian States must be curtailed if unity is to be secured; the second is that history shows this object to have been frequently

HISTORY AS A SCIENCE

attained by the institution of a strong central government ; the third is that it is permissible to copy the
methods by which in past history this result has been
brought about. It will hardly be believed that not one
of these points is discussed in Lord Morley's essay. The
nearest approach is in his unfriendly and inadequate
comment upon the last chapter of *The Prince*, which
contains the keynote of the whole mystery and is therefore the most important in the work. " The last chapter
of *The Prince* is an eloquent appeal to the representation of the House of Medici to heal the bruises and bind
up the wounds of his torn and enslaved country. The
view has been taken that this last chapter has nothing
to do with the fundamental ideas of the book . . . that
it was an afterthought dictated partly by Machiavelli's
personal hopes. . . . The balance of argument seems
on the whole to lean this way." [1] No better instance
could be adduced of the power of the educational bias
to distort the significance of plain facts.

Lord Morley knew that Bacon was attracted by
Machiavelli. " It was natural for that vast and com-
prehensive mind to admire the extension to the sphere
of civil government of the same method that he was
advocating in the investigation of external nature."
Yet though he quotes Bacon's penetrating remark that
" We are much beholden to Machiavelli and others that
wrote what men do and not what they ought to do,"
this does not put him on the track of the true explanation. He did not see the truth for the simple reason
that he did not wish to see it. Hardly anyone, indeed,
could be better qualified for miscomprehension than
Lord Morley, belonging as he does to a sect with whom
the worship of liberty is the beginning and end of political righteousness. To admit Machiavelli's honesty would
be to admit that his indictment of the republican system
in Italy was correct, a conclusion too distasteful to be

[1] Essay on Machiavelli : Morley's *Miscellanies*, Vol. 1, p. 29.

FROM THE POINT OF VIEW OF CONDUCT 117

contemplated. When once Machiavelli had given it as his opinion that the welfare of Italy was incompatible with the separate liberty of the various republics of which it was composed, his condemnation was inevitable. After such blasphemy as this, what need of any further witness? Accordingly, Lord Morley, who pretends to chide the public for its indiscriminating condemnation of Machiavelli, forthwith joins the throng of his detractors, and under cover of an apparently frank and open discussion conducted in the friendliest spirit, manages with a quite " Machiavellian " ingenuity to add to the obloquy with which the unfortunate historian has been overwhelmed.

One more instance of this prejudice may be given. Dispassionate readers of *The Prince* will remember the almost pathetic tone of the dedication to Lorenzo as the one man capable of achieving Italian unity. This is Lord Morley's comment: " So he dedicated his book to Lorenzo in the hope that such speaking proof of experience and capacity would induce those who had destroyed the freedom of the city to give him public employment. His suppleness did not pay!"[1] The attempt to undermine that cardinal tenet of the radical creed that liberty must always, and under all circumstances, bring happiness, was more than Lord Morley could endure. Though the blessings of freedom involved the prevalence of strife throughout the length and breadth of the peninsula, though the air was thick with plottings and counter-plottings, though hardly a year passed without either the devastating incursion of some foreign power or the bloody attack of one free and independent kingdom upon another, we are nevertheless bidden to regard Machiavelli's patriotic desire to cure these evils merely as a time-serving device to get employment!

Pollock, in his *Science of Politics*,[2] though he shows

[1] p. 12.   [2] p. 45.

118 HISTORY AS A SCIENCE

greater comprehension, also fails to perceive that Machiavelli's argument is based upon inductive evidence drawn from all history: "Machiavelli . . . despaired of a strong stable republican government in the Italian states as he knew them. The one pressing need for the restoration of prosperity to Italy was to deliver her from the invaders, French, German and Spanish, who spoiled and ruined her: and this could be done as it seemed to Machiavelli only by some Italian Prince, wiser and more fortunate and more nobly ambitious than others, making himself the chief power in Italy, and gathering such strength of native arms as would enable him to withstand the foreigner." He goes on to add: "For an end so sacred in Italian eyes *all political means of the time* were justified." That, however, is not the point. It was not from a study of political means of contemporary times but of all times that Machiavelli drew the justification for the procedure which he advocated. It was because inductive observation shows these means to have been almost habitually adopted throughout the history of the world that Machiavelli conceived that he had a warrant for the advice which he pressed upon Lorenzo. Scientific warrant he undoubtedly had, but not a moral warrant, and it is in consequence of his failure to perceive that the two were not identical that all the trouble has arisen.

In such matters there is all the difference between the use of the indicative and the use of the imperative. Let us suppose that Machiavelli had never existed, but that history had nevertheless taken such a course as to induce some great man to carry out a policy identical with that suggested by the historian of Florence. And let us suppose that what has happened in other cases happened here also, as it easily might have done, and that a united Italy had emerged great and glorious under the ægis of a mighty chief. Will anyone for a moment maintain that if the conduct of our supposed

FROM THE POINT OF VIEW OF CONDUCT 119

great man had issued in the way suggested, it would have been criticized with a tenth of the indignation which has been expended in denouncing Machiavelli's *Prince*? No; Lorenzo, or whoever he might have been, would have taken his place alongside of Cæsar, Augustus, Vespasian, and the rest. As in other cases, the eyes of historians and of the world would have been fixed on the beneficence of the result with such satisfaction as to lead them to ignore or pardon or extenuate the unpleasant features of the method by which it had been brought about. No doubt visionaries would always have been found to maintain that a free Italy, an Italy, that is to say, ferociously divided against itself, and incessantly trampled beneath the foot of the foreign invader, was a pleasanter and more ennobling spectacle than an Italy which owed tranquillity and prosperity to measures which were, at the outset, unconstitutional. Some Italian Tacitus might no doubt have arisen to lament the departure of the good old days when freedom to wage incessant war upon one another was the glorious privilege of these sovereign states. But the general verdict would have acclaimed Lorenzo as a second Constantine.

The conclusion, according to the present point of view, is as follows: It has to be admitted that though Machiavelli, from the point of view of science, had historical warrant, carefully collated from the various ages, for the course which he proposed to pursue, he nevertheless made a grievous error when he proposed to act upon that warrant. It is at this point that the inductive method, as applied to history, parts company from the inductive method as applied to any other science. Though the historian has a right to investigate his data after the strictest scientific methods and indeed, according to the present theory, is under an obligation to do so, at the next step he must pause. The guardian of conduct with a flaming sword intervenes and asserts that moral reasons alone must decide upon the

120 HISTORY AS A SCIENCE

uses to which the scientific study of history must be put. The mysterious power which makes for righteousness stands ready to enforce its laws against the practice of the universe itself. Machiavelli's case will ever remain to mark the limits which condition the employment of the inductive method in the study of political evolution.

In order to illustrate the present argument the reader has been asked to consider the difference of the verdict which would have been passed in the imaginary case of some great statesman actually securing the unity of Italy in the way suggested by Machiavelli. Yet, after all, there is a modern instance lying ready to hand in the recent history of Germany. The life of Germany's greatest statesman will, in fact, be found especially interesting from this point of view because of the curiously close parallel between the practice of Bismarck and the principles of Machiavelli ; because, in short, Bismarck carried out (short of actual murder) in the nineteenth century what Machiavelli merely recommended in the sixteenth.

The resemblance is not fanciful, nor is the comparison made for literary effect : it is justified if we allow for the slightly different conditions of the sixteenth and nineteenth centuries, and the different part played by the two principals. Like Machiavelli, Bismarck perceived that the great need of his country was unity : the relation of the German states to one another, like the relation of the Italian republics, had proved in the past, though not quite to the same extent, a continual source of national weakness and danger. Bismarck, too, perceived that the necessary union could only be achieved through the agency of a strong ruler, who would not shrink from the necessary measures, including an unjust war ; and that strong ruler he knew to be himself. On a celebrated occasion he explained his intentions to Disraeli, and the words he used read exactly as if he

FROM THE POINT OF VIEW OF CONDUCT 121

and Machiavelli derived their ideas from a common source : " As soon as the army shall have been brought into such a condition as to inspire respect, I shall seize the first best pretext to declare war against Austria, dissolve the German Diet, subdue the minor states and give national unity to Germany under Prussian leadership." The course which Machiavelli urged upon Lorenzo Bismarck undertook himself, and except for this the cases are exactly parallel. The views of Machiavelli were " real-politik " ; and the " real-politik " which Bismarck and his successors openly professed is nothing else than statesmanship modelled upon an inductive study of history.

In this misuse of the inductive method it is noticeable that German historians are also very adept. From the time of Mommsen they have been distinguished from those of any other country by the fact that many of them have deliberately subordinated the study of history to the art of politics. Though they are a nation devoted to scientific research for its own sake, their aim in this case has been not so much to develop the science of history as to instruct their fellow-countrymen and especially their rulers in certain national habits and policies which history shows to have been conducive to the assertion of national supremacy. With a bias peculiarly German they allowed their study of history to persuade them that the imposition by Germany of a world-domination was desirable in the interests of civilization, and that the attainment of this object authorized the use of any means that had historical warrant. When the inductive method in history is thus adapted to political ends there follows, as we have seen, complete indifference to moral considerations. Bismarck, indeed, openly asserted that he thought himself justified in following what we may call evolutional practice rather than moral principle. He had, in fact, as he has himself told us, " settled all that with his Maker." Accordingly he

122 HISTORY AS A SCIENCE

forced the wars of 1866 and 1870, gained an overwhelming victory first over the Austrians and then over the French, and thus made himself master over a united Germany and the dictator of Europe.

Encouraged by these initial successes the Germans began to make an industry of war, and to assert both by precept and practice that it was the most important industry of all; and they did not conceal their belief that it was merely from weakness and cowardice that other nations, especially the English, shrank from following their example. In so doing they assumed that a procedure which would be warranted in physical science, that of imitating any natural process which seems to promise advantage, was equally permissible in political science; and their failure to win the war of 1914, a war which in their opinion was politically and historically justified, was largely due to the fact that moral reprobation for their policy banded the nations of the world against them.

There is another side, however, to the question of realism in politics, and no discussion of the relation of history to political conduct would be complete which did not take it into consideration. Though we cannot accept the inductive study of history as an unconditional guide to political practice, neither can statesmen afford to ignore its teaching altogether, since national existence depends upon its recognition. Yet English liberals and radicals for the last hundred and forty years seem to have prided themselves upon acting in complete disregard of some of the most emphatic lessons of history.

Since the time of Charles James Fox the liberals have regarded it as their mission in life to improve the morality not merely of their own country but of the whole world by upholding ideals of international conduct, which, if practised by an isolated nation would be not only impracticable but ruinous; while the conservatives have been equally determined to be guided by observation

FROM THE POINT OF VIEW OF CONDUCT 123

of international conditions as they are, to avoid all dangerous illusions, and to be content with the more modest aim of ensuring the welfare and safety of their own nation. As elsewhere pointed out[1] Liberalism helps to form a political blend necessary for the proper development of national character. But the claim of the liberals to grateful recognition on this account would be more impressive if they had not by their deliberate policy on more than one occasion endangered the very existence of the nation, which may undoubtedly be said to owe its preservation to the strong common sense of their opponents, whose aim has always been to keep their statesmanship in touch with the realities of actual political existence.

This disastrous tendency in liberal policy has been apparent since 1770; it was a contributory cause of our defeat in the struggle with the rebellious American colonies; and later on very nearly ensured the triumph of Napoleon; while the influence it exerted between 1870 and 1914 helped to precipitate the most terrible war in history upon a nation not only materially but morally unprepared. During that period Gladstone, Harcourt, Campbell-Bannerman, Morley and their followers made a merit of ignoring the unpleasant features of international life and of acting as if they did not exist. It is, in fact, plain that the fallacies of the educational theory, and especially the dangerous tendency to assume that things are as you wish them to be, may beguile not only historians but politicians—in the latter case to the peril of the national existence, since an attitude which is comparatively harmless in the study may be fatal in the council chamber. The educational system in politics overlooks the truth that the indulgence in political idealism, however ennobling in theory, is commendable in practice only so far as it is consistent with national safety. Since 1870 Lord Rosebery has been

[1] *Conditions of National Success.*

HISTORY AS A SCIENCE

the solitary statesman on the liberal side who had a clear appreciation of international realities, and his patriotic attempt to introduce sanity into the councils of his party was the real cause of his practically enforced retirement.

In contrast, then, to Bismarck and the German rulers who may be said to have followed too closely the inductive study of history we have the English liberal party who have paid no attention to it at all. A judicious blending of political idealism and political realism issuing in a foreign policy adapted to the requirements of the international situation is obviously the attitude for true statesmanship to adopt.

So far we have dealt with the contradictory requirements of knowledge and conduct in the sphere of politics. But the discrepancy between the spirit which we must adopt to gain a scientific knowledge of social tendencies and the spirit which should animate us in our actual relations with our fellow-creatures is shown in an equally striking manner in another department of history, that of economics. In the controversy which has arisen over the so-called science of political economy we find the principle once more emphasized that we are not permitted to approach a human problem from the purely intellectual side alone, and that the stern attitude which is necessary for the ascertainment of truth must be humanized and moralized when we come to deal with real life. As in politics so in economics, the observation of the course of nature in the past is one thing, the application of the results so obtained is another. While on the one hand we can only gain the requisite knowledge by a purely intellectual study of the phenomena, undeterred by any regard for the possible effect of such knowledge upon conduct, yet if we presume to utilize our information regardless of moral or social considerations, the conscience of mankind at once proceeds to issue an emphatic protest.

Whatever the deficiencies of the study of political

FROM THE POINT OF VIEW OF CONDUCT   125

economy it has at least been more successful from the scientific point of view than any other branch of social investigation. It is, in fact, the only department of human life about which certain generally-accepted laws have been formulated and certain relatively reliable conclusions have been reached. And what is still more noticeable, the methods which have secured this comparative success are the very methods which have met with the most unsparing condemnation from philanthropists. It is precisely because political economists allowed themselves to become absorbed in the intellectual side of their problem to the exclusion of disturbing humanitarian considerations that they were able to make progress. They obtained their success because they studied their phenomena with a greater degree of scientific detachment than has been employed in dealing with any other aspect of human life. After a preliminary survey of the facts in a strictly inductive manner, certain provisional conclusions were formed with regard to economic needs and the way in which they were supplied. By use of a hypothesis, which humanly speaking was a fiction, but which was nevertheless extremely useful as a scientific device, the hypothesis of the " Economic man," political economists were enabled to enunciate certain propositions which were both true and valuable.

But if it was this scientific indifference to the sentimental aspect of their subject which gave to political economists better results than were obtained in any other branch of social studies, it is impossible to ignore the cost at which their success was gained. The attitude necessary to achieve this success was, from the humane point of view, so heartless that the conscience of the community was revolted. Almost from the first a protest was entered by certain leading thinkers or moralists against the inhumanity of the " dismal science," that is to say, against the spirit in which the study of political economy was conducted. And still the contro-

HISTORY AS A SCIENCE

versy rages as to how far the human aspect of economic relations should be allowed to modify the conclusions warranted by an exact study of the facts.

The solution of this difficulty lies in the considerations already brought forward. Political economists are perfectly right in studying their subject as they do and in forming the conclusions which inductive observation warrants, provided that they submit those conclusions to the verdict of morality before they proceed to act upon them. The adoption of the passionless attitude is justified so long as it is restricted to the sole purpose of gaining knowledge. It is because they unwittingly overlooked this aspect of the matter that the economists brought themselves into disrepute.

The first and most striking general fact revealed by the study of political economy is the brutal pressure of economic laws or tendencies upon certain classes who, for no fault of their own, have been involved in their operation. From the scientific point of view these laws are undoubtedly true laws; if things are left to themselves they come into inexorable operation. The *laissez-faire* policy may even at one time have been the only method of promoting industrial efficiency. But the effect of unrestricted competition upon the well-being of the lower orders was so terrible that the conscience of the community gradually insisted upon counteracting and regulating measures.

It is over the question of these counteracting measures that the dispute has been and is most bitter. Economists at one time asserted the existence of an iron law of wages which tended to keep the remuneration of the worker at the level of subsistence. If we allow ourselves to be guided entirely by a study of the past it is undoubtedly true that an economic tendency is to be observed which keeps the wages of unskilled labour at the lowest point at which existence can be maintained. To insist that such a tendency is unalterable,

FROM THE POINT OF VIEW OF CONDUCT 127

like a law of physics or chemistry, is to overlook a vital distinction. The laws of physics or chemistry do not change because the data remains the same. There is, for instance, no power which can alter the properties of atoms. But the data of political or economic science do not remain the same; certain influences are at work which definitely alter their "properties." These so-called data are, in fact, human beings with intellects to perceive and hearts to feel. Education and religion are the powers which are continually changing them. When by means of education the sense of moral obligation has been increased, the whole aspect of the case is altered to such an extent that it is no longer possible to treat the results of inductive observation as yielding principles upon which we may safely proceed to act. Those who were in the habit of speaking as if economic laws possessed an unalterable power overlooked this consideration. They forgot that such laws are laws no longer when the human conscience is stirred, but are subject to revision, sometimes even to abrogation, in the moral and social interests of the human race.

Accordingly the humanitarians, disregarding the scientific strength of their opponents' case, and being entirely justified from the moral point of view in so doing, succeeded in throwing grave discredit upon reasoning which seemed to countenance such unpalatable conclusions. Yet the method of the political economists was from the scientific point of view correct. Because the existence of certain tendencies which they showed to be in operation was at one time held to justify the exploitation of the wage-earning classes, the science itself is not on that account to be blamed. It is the illegitimate use to which the conclusions were put, not the fact that they were formulated, which is open to criticism. The case of political economy is, in fact, the exact reverse of the case of history. While history has failed because

128 HISTORY AS A SCIENCE

historians have allowed their intellectual perceptions to be blinded by their moral and political sympathies, the study of economics has succeeded because the opposite policy was followed, and moral and humanitarian sentiment was not allowed to interfere with the business of formulating conclusions.

And the lesson which we are taught in either case is the same. Those human feelings which we must discard when we seek for knowledge we must as carefully retain both in economics and politics when we contemplate action. Machiavelli pointed to history and said: " This is how the patriotic ruler must act if he wishes to put an end to the evils of anarchy. It is true that the process will involve bloodshed, but the records of the past show that national unity is cheap at the price." The early economists also pointed to history and said: " This is how the employer must act if he wishes to produce the greatest amount of national wealth : such action may involve hardship to those living on the margin of subsistence, but it is the only method of procuring that abundant supply of cheap labour which is necessary for economic prosperity ; the unpleasantness entailed is an inevitable part of the constitution of the universe." If economic laws are like the laws of the inorganic world, then the employers were justified in denouncing interference with a natural process which, though it entailed hardship, immensely cheapened commodities. But since the time of Owen and Carlyle and Ruskin the conviction has gradually triumphed that a system which secures economy of production at the cost of the moral and physical degradation of the labourer is a disgrace to civilized humanity.

It was this last consideration which gave rise to a movement upon which the attention of the world is concentrated at the present day. Socialism from the evolutional point of view may in fact be regarded as a natural corrective to those inhuman aspects of political

FROM THE POINT OF VIEW OF CONDUCT 129

economy which have been criticized in the preceding pages. Its genesis is as follows : Science investigating the laws of the production and distribution of wealth had found that though certain industrial conditions bore with especial severity upon the wage-earning class, those conditions had to be endured because they were natural and also greatly increased the wealth of the nation. The consequence was that in the early days of the " industrial revolution " at the beginning of last century deplorable atrocities were sanctioned under the plea that the general economic interests of the community could not otherwise be assured. Indeed, the belief that the poverty of the working classes was inevitable not only commended itself to selfish manufacturers, but practically to the whole radical party, including men who considered themselves emancipated leaders of political thought such as John Bright. Presently, however, resolute moralists were heard denouncing the flagrant inhumanity of unregulated industrialism, and disputing the belief in the necessary permanence of conditions which were an outrage on moral decency. Such opinions, at first but little regarded, gradually became formed into a school of thought called socialism, which asserted not merely that the economic man was a fiction, but that most of the so-called economic laws were equally imaginary, or at least that they were indefinitely alterable in such a way as to secure the happiness and prosperity of all.

From the practical point of view the socialistic ideals of the reorganization of industry as at present formulated may be regarded as Utopian dreams, because they postulate the harmonious presence of absolutely contradictory qualities in the character of the individual. To carry socialistic theories into practice men must simultaneously display all the energy which springs from self-interest, and all the kindliness which inspires self-renunciation. It is assumed that those efforts which have

130 HISTORY AS A SCIENCE

hitherto been made by the vast majority of mankind only under the stimulus of gain, ambition or dire necessity, efforts indispensable for national prosperity, will continue to be made with the same or with even greater energy under a socialistic system which has deliberately eliminated these motives. Not a particle of real proof of the feasibility of such a scheme has ever been forthcoming, all actual experiments having ended in utter failure. On these grounds most people not unnaturally condemn socialistic theories as not merely useless but pernicious, tending to the complete disorganization of society without any compensating advantage. This view, however, in spite of its apparent reasonableness is not altogether justified. Such movements may have an importance not readily to be inferred from the unreasonable nature of the doctrines put forward. According to the present theory, the spread of socialism is due to a tendency of a perfectly natural kind, extravagant certainly, but natural because it is extravagant.

In a previous work [1] the theory was maintained that the life of a nation can only be a healthy life on condition that the conflicting interests of the State and of the individual receive relatively equal attention; that these interests for the last hundred and fifty years of English history have been championed by the conservatives on the one side and by the liberals or radicals on the other; and the view was expressed that the natural development of English political life would lead the nation in the direction of a coalition government which would secure in a more systematic manner that fusion of principles necessary for the well-being of the State which was formerly obtained by the open rivalry of antagonistic parties. The first coalition government did not last long, but it has been succeeded in 1931 by another coalition government which, under a much more acceptable and appropriate name seems well calculated to

[1] *Conditions of National Success.*

FROM THE POINT OF VIEW OF CONDUCT 131

secure that harmonious adjustment of divergent aims necessary to the well-being of the Empire.

Meanwhile, should the community not prove sufficiently sane-minded to retain the idea of a national government, and should the socialists one day return to office, this is a contingency which need not be greatly feared provided that one most important condition is secured. Their demands must be reduced to moderate dimensions by a strong parliamentary and national opposition. On this understanding a leaven of socialism in the political composition need not be feared. The fusion of principles which was formerly secured by the opposition between conservatives and radicals would then be secured by the opposition between conservatives and socialists. The socialists are the lineal political descendants of the radicals, and their appearance need cause no great apprehension since it betokens that the evolution of the idea of the State is proceeding on harmonious lines in the following way: However much liberals may repudiate connection with the doctrines and principles of socialism, it remains true that socialism is merely the liberal idea of the importance of the individual carried to its logical conclusion. Though radicals like John Bright furiously opposed the " feudal tyranny " of their own social and political superiors, they had no real sympathy for the class below them, since they were at the same time content to leave the working man to the tender mercies of the Factory System. And whereas liberals and radicals, generally speaking, assumed that the winning of political liberty by the individual was sufficient to assure the welfare of the State, socialists held that the championship of the rights of the individual is not complete until he is protected from economic as well as political injustice.

Accordingly, we may conclude that though the delusions with which socialism is permeated might seem to discredit it as a rational theory, it has nevertheless a definite and important place in the scheme of social

HISTORY AS A SCIENCE

evolution, though not exactly that which its supporters claim for it. It comes as a protest against the too rigid system of economics, of which we have already spoken, which left considerations of humanity almost entirely out of sight. Whereas the founders of the science of political economy took nothing into account except methods of wealth-producing efficiency, entirely disregarding any hardship that might be entailed by the operation of economic laws, socialists on the other hand go to the opposite extreme, making the happiness of the manual labourer almost the sole consideration, asserting the immediate possibility of the equal diffusion of wealth, and attributing all the evils of modern economic existence entirely to the tyranny of those who have control of the means of production. They take their stand on the belief that economic and social life can, by the enactment of the proper regulations, be made exactly what we wish, and that all assertions to the contrary are inspired merely by the greed and selfishness of the employing classes.

But though it is not true that the laws of the production and distribution of national wealth necessitate the existence of a labouring class perpetually on the verge of starvation, neither can we accept the magic vision of universal well-being which rises at the touch of the socialistic wand. The economic dispute, in fact, seems to be following the normal course of all such controversies, where exaggeration on the one side is met by exaggeration on the other, and progress is affected by the adjustment of the rival points of view. To the gloomy conception of a world largely condemned to toil and privation, socialists oppose the prospect of an almost limitless individual happiness. Between these two opposing theories that economic laws are immutable and that they are capable of indefinite modification a middle course will be found, and by the adjustment of these rival points of view a more satisfactory condition of

FROM THE POINT OF VIEW OF CONDUCT 133

industrial relations will be secured. The socialist will come to recognize that other causes besides the sinister designs of the capitalist have been answerable for the hardships of the labouring classes, while the scientific believer in economic law will be brought to admit the possibility of a more equitable distribution of wealth. Socialism, in short, is apparently one of those evolutional tendencies which is destined to alter human conditions, not by securing its own demands, but by modifying the attitude of its opponents. Though its tenets as they stand are impossible of realization, yet if regarded merely as a corrective to the evils of unfettered industrialism, they may well be necessary to the future of civilization.

We find, then, as a result of the inquiry which has been conducted in the preceding pages of this chapter that we cannot make a direct application either to politics or to economics of the knowledge gained by the inductive study of history. But though some of the lessons of history cannot be directly applied to human purposes this does not make its scientific study any the less necessary. Observation of the methods of nature in other departments leaves not the slightest doubt that in politics as in economics there are certain main lines of development in accordance with which alone can improvement be successfully attempted. All innovations which fail to take account of this truth are doomed to be worse than useless.

The chief lesson to be learned is this, that though the social structure may be altered in detail it cannot be altered in fundamental design. It is the office of the science of history to learn the outlines of this fundamental design, even if the knowledge so gained is valuable in a negative rather than in a positive way, and assists progress not so much by telling us what to do as what not to do. At least one half of the usual socialistic programme may be regarded as altogether unattainable ;

HISTORY AS A SCIENCE

and even if the attainment of the other half be possible in the distant future, it will not be by the methods at present advocated by the most " advanced " reformers. It is the practice of commanders in war, when meditating an important offensive, to try the enemy's front in order to discover where it is possible to break through. The scientific inquiry into political and social conditions should be similarly directed with the object of ascertaining at what point and in what way the attempt can best be made to amend the hardships and injustices of the original process of social and economic evolution. While some so-called laws of nature are modifiable, others are not, and it is essential to know which belong to either category. The indispensable condition of success in social, political and economic reform is that any changes which are made in the existing order of things must harmonize with pre-existing evolutional tendencies ; and only a knowledge of the laws of progress gained by inductive observation, will enable this condition to be fulfilled. A rich and promising harvest awaits the use of the inductive method in history. If, as a survey of the cosmic process seems to suggest, the intervention of the human intellect is necessary to complete the process of human evolution, and if interference with the laws of nature is part of the course of nature, it is only after an inductive study of history that the task can be properly performed.

INDEX

A

Ability in government, 45, 46, 101, 102
Absolute government, 23, 41, 44, 45 *et pass.*
Acton, Lord, 27, 28, 39
" Admiral of the Atlantic," 74
Advancement of knowledge, 1
America, 73–8, 123
Anarchy, 91–4, 104–6
Antagonism of Societies, 58, 59 *et pass.*
Antonines, 40
Aristotle, 96
Art and science of politics, 111, 112, 128
Athenians, 3, 44
Author's scheme in present and preceding works, 6, 32–5
Average historian, views of, 9, 10

B

Bacon, 116
Barbaroux, 84
Berthier, 83
Birrell, 13
Bismarck, 120–2
Bright, 129, 131
British Empire, 70–4, 78
British Fascisti, 109, 110
Burke, 92
Bury, 13

C

Campbell-Bannerman, 123
Carlyle, 18, 27, 84, 86, 88, 97
Carr, H. W., 4
Charnwood, Lord, 78
Churchill, Winston, 71
Coalition Government, 130, 131
Comte, Auguste, 23, 27
Conception and preconception in history, 26, 116, 117
Conflicting tendencies, 1, 130, 132
Congress and legislation, 54
Constitutional history, 48–52
— ideas out of place, 21, 39–41
Cook, 106
Corcyrean revolution, 90
Crowd, psychology of, 61, 95–7, 106

D

Danton, 83, 84
Darwin, 2, 5, 89
Data of history more than adequate, 29, 30
" Dismal Science," the, 125–8
Double appeal of history, 9

E

" Economic man," 125
Edward II, 51
England, 70, 71, 72

135

136 HISTORY AS A SCIENCE

F

Factory system, 131
Fascisti, 108–10
Fouillon, 83
France, 66, 68–74
Frederick the Great, 90
Freeman, 14, 21
French Revolution, 82–98
Froude, 22
Future form of history, 35–7

G

Galba, 41
General Strike, 105, 107
Germany, 60, 66–73, 90
Gibbon, 40
Gladstone, 123
Gooch, Dr., 13, 14, 20–3, 27, 29, 30
Government, 38–55
— evolution of, 33, 34 *et pass.*
Grand Duchess Elizabeth, 100
Great War, causes of, 70–3
Green, J. R., 21
Guedalla, 36
Guicciardini, 26

H

Harcourt, 123
Harrison, Frederick, 12, 19–20, 56, 84
Hearnshaw, Professor, 107
Historians, double allegiance of, 6–9 *et pass.*
— victims of convention, 10
History, schools of, 13
— scientific and narrative, 35–7
— universal appeal of, 9
Hitler, 67
Huxley, 2
Hypothesis, use of, 29–32, 58

I

Illuminati, 89, 90
Inductive study of history, 32–5 *et pass.*
Industrial revolution, 126–9
Insatiability of expectation in revolution, 95–100
Interference with nature, 18, 133, 4
Isolation of important phenomena, 14, 31, 33
Italy, 68
Italy and Machiavelli, 114–19

J

Jurists' view of war, 58–60

K

Kerensky, 106
Knowledge, function of, 14–16

L

Laissez-faire, 126
League of Nations, 64, 65, 68, 78–81
Le Bon, 61
Legislation in America, 54
Liberal policy, 71, 122–4
Liberty, 21, 42, 45, 46, 48
Lilley, 27
Lloyd George, 93, 100
Locke, 38, 39
Lorenzo, 118, 119
Louis XVI, 92, 97, 103, 105, 106

M

Macaulay, 12, 18, 37
Machiavelli, 113–21, 128
Mahan, 29, 30
Maitland, 50–2
Mann, 108

INDEX

137

Marat, 84
Marseillais, the, 84
Mass psychology and war, 61–4
Metaphysicians, 42, 43
Mirabeau, 83, 90, 100–2, 108
Mommsen, 22
Monroe doctrine, 74
Moral philosophy, 46–8
Morality of nations, 62, 63, 80
Morley, Lord, 25–9, 39, 45–56, 84, 86, 88, 92, 93, 96, 115–117
Muse and method of history, 36, 37
Mussolini, 65, 108

N

National success, 34, 35
Nationality, advantages of, 80, 81
Nations and individuals, 64
Niebuhr, 22

O

Observation, deficiencies of, 39–41
— duty of, 6, 7, 43, 52, 55
Orleanist conspiracy, 83, 89, 90
Owen, 128

P

Parliament, 46, 51–4
Political economy, 123–8, 132
Pollock, 118
Polybius, 13
Prince, the, of Machiavelli, 113–17
" Progressive desire," 95–7
Prussia, 89, 90
Psychology of nations, 61, 63, 79

Psychology of revolution, 89–97, 106
— of war, 56

R

Ranke, 13, 22
Reade, Winwood, 112
" Real-politik," 121
Reveillon, 83
Richelieu, 102
Roland, Madame, 83, 84, 95
Rosebery, Lord, 123–4
Ruskin, 27
Russia, 68, 100, 104

S

St. Etienne, 90
St. Just, 97
Schools of history, 13, 14
Science of history, 16–18
Seeley, Sir J., 12, 13, 29, 30, 53, 54
Selection, principle of, 27
September massacres, 84, 87
Sismondi, 21
Socialism, 128–34
Social organism, 4, 24, 57–9, 75, 79
Sociology, study of, 23–5
Spencer, Herbert, 25, 27
Stubbs, 14
Sully, 92, 93

T

Thiers, 21
Thucydides, 8, 18, 88–91
Times, The, on Fascism, 109
Trades Disputes Act, 107
— Union Act, 107
Trevelyan, G. M., 31

138 HISTORY AS A SCIENCE

Tristram, Canon, 5
Turgot, 26
Turkey, 65
Tyranny, 41, 50

V

Verification, 31, 32
Victorian attitude to knowledge, 3, 15
Von der Goltz, 90

W

War, causes of, 58–60, 63
— inveteracy of, 86–9
— psychology of, 56, 61
— and social organism, 25, 56
War of Independence, 76, 77
Webster, Mrs. Nesta, 82–100
Weishaupt, 90
Wilson, President, 60, 61
World supremacy and Germany, 70

Made and Printed in Great Britain by Butler & Tanner Ltd., Frome and London